MY POCKET
POSITIVITY

ANYTIME EXERCISES THAT BOOST
OPTIMISM, CONFIDENCE, AND POSSIBILITY

COURTNEY E. ACKERMAN

ADAMS MEDIA
NEW YORK   LONDON   TORONTO   SYDNEY   NEW DELHI

Adams Media
An Imprint of Simon & Schuster, Inc.
57 Littlefield Street
Avon, Massachusetts 02322

First Adams Media trade paperback edition November 2018

ADAMS MEDIA and colophon are trademarks of Simon & Schuster.

For information about special discounts for bulk purchases, please contact Simon &
Schuster Special Sales at 1-866-506-1949 or business@simonandschuster.com.

The Simon & Schuster Speakers Bureau can bring authors to your live event. For more
information or to book an event contact the Simon & Schuster Speakers Bureau at
1-866-248-3049 or visit our website at www.simonspeakers.com.

Interior design by Heather McKiel
Interior images © Getty Images/hpkalyani

Manufactured in China

10 9 8 7 6 5 4 3 2

Library of Congress Cataloging-in-Publication Data
Ackerman, Courtney E., author.
My pocket positivity / Courtney E. Ackerman.
Avon, Massachudetts: Adams Media, 2018.
Series: My pocket.
LCCN 2018017349 | ISBN 9781507208502 (pb) | ISBN 9781507208519 (ebook)
Subjects: LCSH: Self-actualization (Psychology) | Motivation (Psychology) |
Self-confidence. | BISAC: SELF-HELP / Motivational & Inspirational. | SELF-HELP /
Personal Growth / General.
Classification: LCC BF637.S4 A345 2018 | DDC 158.1--dc23
LC record available at https://lccn.loc.gov/2018017349

ISBN 978-1-5072-0850-2
ISBN 978-1-5072-0851-9 (ebook)

CONTENTS

INTRODUCTION

* *Are you looking for a more vibrant and happy life?*
* *Do you want to boost your confidence and enhance all that is special about you?*
* *Are you looking to banish negativity and find a fresh perspective?*

If so, the answer you're looking for is *positivity*!

My Pocket Positivity presents 140 exercises you can do at home, at work, or on the go to help you make the most of potentially bad situations, see the best in other people, and view yourself and your abilities in a positive light. These quick but powerful exercises will help you become more mindful, more grateful, and a better, more optimistic version of yourself!

You'll learn how to develop and increase some of the most important positivity traits, including:

* Well-being
* Happiness and inspiration
* Resilience
* Optimism and gratitude
* Self-confidence and self-esteem
* Mindfulness
* Self-love and compassion

As you delve into these exercises, keep in mind that they don't follow a strict order. If you feel drawn to one topic in particular, skip straight to it. The rest will be here waiting for you whenever you are ready. After all, there is no wrong way to go about building a happier, more positive life! A brighter, better future is waiting for you, so turn the page and let's get started!

CHAPTER 1

EXERCISES TO ENHANCE WELL-BEING

There is a good reason that the first chapter in this book is dedicated to helping you enhance your well-being. Well-being is more than happiness or just feeling good—it's a global sense that your life is a good one, that you are fulfilled and satisfied by your day-to-day life.

A high level of well-being is the foundation upon which you can build the life that you want, and it can open you up to developing your gratitude, optimism, confidence, happiness, and other important, positive traits. Having at least a minimum level of well-being is vital to living the good life, and the exercises in this chapter can help you get to the minimum and beyond.

PAY IT FORWARD

The effectiveness of this exercise hinges on the natural human desire to help others. Doing good for others is one of the best ways to enhance your own well-being, and thinking about the potential ripple effects of your positive actions can boost it even more!

Engaging in this exercise is easy. You don't need to donate all your money or volunteer all your extra time to gain the benefits of altruism; all you need to do is one helpful or generous thing for someone else.

Think about something someone did for you, something touching and unexpected. It might be hard to think of it at first, but some act of kindness will eventually come to you. Maybe a cashier alerted you to a discount or coupon that you didn't know about, or maybe someone let you take their cab when you were in a hurry.

Take a moment to think about how it felt to be on the receiving end of this action. Cultivate gratitude for this random act of kindness.

Then, pay it forward! Give up your seat on the subway, bake cookies for a new neighbor, pay for someone's coffee in the drive-through, or just give a stranger a heartfelt compliment.

What you do is not important, as long as it is a positive act that is intended to brighten someone else's day. Engage in small acts of kindness as often as you can, and you'll notice a marked increase in your own well-being!

TAKE A WALK

As simple as it sounds, taking a walk can give you a surprisingly big boost to your well-being, both physically and mentally. It's a simple and easy activity that almost anyone can do when they want to feel better.

The next time you are feeling sad, anxious, sluggish, unfocused, or upset, put on your walking shoes and go outside. If you're low on energy, try a quick, vigorous walk to put some pep into your day. A quick-stepping stroll will invigorate and energize you, leaving you with newfound motivation to carry on with your day.

If you're feeling overwhelmed or you've been multitasking all day, try a slow, purposeful walk. Force yourself to take a few medium steps instead of several small steps or one giant stride. While you walk, remind yourself to look around you and enjoy the scenery. Notice any particularly appealing sights, for example, a tree with leaves waving gently in the breeze or a happy couple walking arm in arm down the street.

Whichever kind of walk you decide to take, keep some of your focus on your breath. Take in deep breaths through your nose, hold them for a moment or two, and let them out steadily through your mouth (for the energetic walk) or your nose (for the mindful walk).

Remember to give yourself a metaphorical pat on the back for engaging in a healthy physical activity, and thank yourself for doing something good for your mind and body.

CHALLENGE YOUR NEGATIVE THOUGHTS

We all have the occasional sneaking negative thought. After all, it's impossible to be happy all the time! It's normal to feel a little down sometimes, but the trouble comes when your negative thoughts start repeating and gaining ground in your mind.

One of the best things you can do for your well-being is to scan your thoughts for those that are negative and challenge them.

First, open yourself up to the thoughts going through your head. It might be difficult to slow them down and catch them—if that's the case, continue on to Chapter 7 and pick up some tips and tricks on developing mindfulness, then come back and try this exercise again.

Once you have identified a negative thought, challenge it by asking yourself these four questions:

1. Is the thought true?
2. Is it even possible to know if it's true?
3. What effects does believing this thought have on me?
4. What are the potential effects of *not* believing this thought?

Your answers to these four questions can guide you to the best way forward. If the thought is not true and is having harmful effects, you can challenge its validity and commit to questioning this thought whenever it arises.

You can use this exercise for every negative thought that pops up (and some overly positive thoughts too).

CREATE A DANCE

Try this easy exercise when you want to boost your sense of well-being and get more in tune with your authentic self.

Stand up and move to a space where you have a lot of room around you to move freely. Take a few moments to think about your current mood.

Ask yourself questions like:

* What's on my mind right now?
* How am I feeling?
* How would I like to feel?

Consider your answers to these questions, and come up with a dance move that expresses who you are and your experience in this moment. There are no rules for this movement, only that it must be in line with how you're feeling.

You can jump, skip, sway, dip, sweep, wiggle, wave, or flail. You can raise your arms, lift your knees, shake a leg, bow forward, lean backward, or do all of these moves in a sequence. You can move slowly or quickly, in a regular or in an erratic pattern, in smooth or in short, brisk movements—whatever matches your authentic self, right here and right now.

Don't worry about how you look. It doesn't matter whether you look graceful, sexy, or skilled in this moment. All that matters is that you are expressing and honoring your current state and your authentic self. When we are in touch with our authentic selves, it's hard *not* to get a boost to our well-being!

FIND PEACE WITH DEEP, MINDFUL BREATHING

This exercise benefits both brain and body. All you need to do is breathe!

1. Sit down in a comfortable chair or on the floor. Get comfortable, but not *too* comfortable. Sit with a straight back and rest your hands on your lap, or place one hand on your chest and the other on your stomach. Close your eyes and just sit for a moment, getting accustomed to how you feel in this position.
2. Take a deep breath in through your mouth or your nose, hold it in your lungs for 1 second, and then exhale deeply. You should fill your lungs completely on the in breath and empty them completely on the out breath.
3. During each breath, pay attention to the feeling of fullness in your chest and the ensuing emptiness when you expel the air. If you have one hand on your chest and the other on your belly, feel the slow, steady rise and fall as you breathe.
4. Continue breathing with this method for 3 minutes, or at least twenty breaths.
5. Once you have finished your deep breathing, think about how you feel now compared with before you began the exercise. Don't be surprised if you feel calmer and more collected after the breaths—this is a common reaction!

You can use this simple well-being exercise anytime, but keep it in mind especially for situations in which you need to find peace or create calm within yourself.

TAKE A RISK

As scary as it can be to try a new activity or step outside of your comfort zone, it's worth the effort. Trying new things and taking small risks is vital to your well-being.

Have you been considering taking a dancing lesson? Do you stare longingly at the happy, healthy people stretching in the yoga studio as you walk by? Are you both excited and terrified by the prospect of signing up for a speed-dating event? Instead of convincing yourself that branching out isn't worth the effort and courage required, challenge yourself to follow through on one of your unfulfilled desires.

Commit to doing at least one new, intimidating thing every day. Taking a risk can be as small as striking up a conversation with someone you don't know or as large as accepting a job offer in a different country. The point of this exercise isn't to radically alter your life, but to develop a habit of trying new things and opening yourself up to all the possibilities that life has to offer.

The next time you find yourself talking your more adventurous side out of accepting an invitation to karaoke night or coming up with excuses to get out of a volunteering opportunity with a friend, stop and ask yourself why you are avoiding something that you might enjoy. If the answer is simply that you are scared to take a risk, push yourself to overcome your fear and dive headfirst into the uncertainty!

WRITE A LETTER TO A LOVED ONE

There are so many benefits to connecting and sharing with the ones you love that it's hard to pin this exercise down to one chapter; however, there is a strong link between healthy relationships and well-being, making it an excellent fit in this one!

Think about a friend or family member with whom you share a meaningful connection. It's best to choose someone you don't see on a regular basis, or someone you rarely have deep, intimate conversations with. Once you have someone in mind, grab a piece of paper and a pen or pencil (or fire up your email account and open a new message) and get ready to write.

Craft a message to your friend or family member following these steps:

1. Make note of at least one thing you love about your friend or family member, and let the person know you appreciate that about him or her.
2. Recall a memory you two share, preferably something deep and meaningful or something silly and funny. Describe it to your friend or family member.
3. End with an invitation to spend time together, either right away at a specific event or place or at a more distant event that you think he or she will enjoy.

Writing this letter offers tons of benefits: it will give you a chance to get your feelings on paper, and it will make your loved one feel good; it also is a gesture that tends to reflect back on the giver after it brightens the receiver's day.

MAKE FUNNY FACES

One of the new trends in looking younger, facial yoga promises to remove a few years' worth of wrinkles from your face; however, it may have a second, unintended benefit—boosting your well-being!

Give these facial yoga moves a try, and let the good feelings flow:

* **The Manual Smile**—Begin by adopting a gentle smile with your lips closed. Purse your lips slightly, then place your pointer and middle fingers on the corners of your mouth and pull the corners up toward your cheekbones. Hold this exaggerated smile for 30 seconds.
* **The Surprise!**—You know the universal "surprised" face? This move draws on that typical wide-eyed look. Open your eyes as wide as you can. Aim to show as much of the white of your eyes as possible, and hold this look for 30 seconds.
* **The Funny Face**—If you've ever tried to make a child laugh, you'll likely recognize this expression. Begin this exercise by putting on your Surprise! expression. Next, draw in a big breath, then blow all the air into your cheeks. Keeping your eyes wide and your mouth closed, alternate puffing out each cheek three times.
* **The Stick Out Your Tongue**—As the name implies, this expression involves only one thing: sticking your tongue out as far as it can go. Hold this pose for 60 seconds.

LEARN SOMETHING NEW

There are so many potential benefits to learning new things. Beyond the obvious advantage of building your knowledge, learning something new can also open you up to fresh and exciting opportunities, give you a rush of feel-good chemicals, and improve your self-confidence and self-esteem.

Cultivating a learning mind-set is a great way to bolster your well-being, and it's surprisingly easy to do. Simply dedicate yourself to learning one new thing every day.

The new thing could be experimenting with a recipe you've never tried before, researching a fun fact about your favorite historical figure, or watching a how-to video on a craft or activity you'd like to try. You could also go for a more involved learning experience by signing up for a class on a new language, a course in a topic outside of your area of expertise, or lessons in playing a musical instrument.

Whether you choose to learn a onetime fact or to develop a long-term skill, you will reap the benefits from learning every day. Building and enhancing your love of learning will keep you open to new experiences and new knowledge, something that is invaluable in our rapidly changing world with its ever-expanding technology and ideas.

You can award yourself bonus "well-being points" for learning something new from a friend, acquaintance, or friendly stranger. When you learn interesting new things from someone, you associate those things with that person, making it easy to lay the foundations for a new friendship or build up an existing one.

EXERCISE YOUR CREATIVITY

Many people don't think they are very creative. Chances are, you're much more creative than you think you are! However, even if you don't think you're a very creative person, you can benefit from engaging in a creativity exercise.

Doing something creative can be an excellent boost to your well-being. It feels good to apply your skills, stretch your abilities, and make something new and original.

This exercise is great because it is so customizable. Are you interested in writing fiction? Put pen to paper and write one chapter, or even just a few pages!

Do you love poetry? Pen a poem.

Are you passionate about graphic design? Create a logo that expresses who you are today, at this very moment.

Is cooking your passion? Take an old standby recipe, and challenge yourself to add at least three new ingredients to totally transform the dish.

The point of this exercise isn't to create something that will win awards or sell books, but to give your creative side a chance to express itself. Don't worry if your creation isn't objectively good; instead, focus on how it makes you feel.

Whenever you need a pick-me-up, switch up your routine by doing something creative. You won't regret it!

LIVE BY YOUR VALUES

A great way to maintain a healthy sense of well-being is to ensure that you are living by your values. A huge source of unhappiness comes from not acting in accordance with your beliefs.

Whenever you are feeling a dip in your well-being, pause and take a moment to consider whether you are living in accordance with your values.

Not sure exactly what your values are? Follow these steps:

1. Think about the times in your life when you were at your most happy, proud of yourself, and fulfilled. Note the circumstances at these times (e.g., what you were doing, who you were with).
2. Identify some of the values that correspond to those circumstances, and come up with a list of five to ten top values (e.g., you were most happy when you finally mastered a difficult skill, meaning that growth is likely an important value for you).

Now that you have a list of your top values, refer to it when you are struggling with self-doubt or unhappiness. You can even laminate the list and carry it with you if that would be helpful.

Ask yourself, "Am I being true to my top values right now? If not, what can I change to be more in line with my top values?"

TAKE A HELICOPTER VIEW

Humans have a tendency to get bogged down in minor annoyances. This is a natural tendency, but one that is not very helpful! Sometimes all you need to do to improve your well-being is to change your perspective. Pull out this exercise when something has you feeling down, upset, or irritated.

1. Identify what is dragging down your mood. Be honest with yourself and avoid self-judgment. Hold the source of your annoyance in your mind, and visualize it in detail if that helps you.
2. Next, imagine getting into a helicopter (metaphorical or physical) and slowly lifting off from the thing that is dragging you down. Watch as it gets smaller and smaller.
3. Once you can hardly see it anymore, look up and around you. What do you see? What is at this higher level of attention?

If your irritation is bad drivers in traffic, taking the helicopter view can show you that there are hundreds or even thousands of people just like you who are also feeling the same aggravation right now. When you look up, you'll see the big picture: that you'll be home sooner or later, and by next week you'll have forgotten all about this irritation.

You can try this for any problem, big or small, silly or serious. There is always a higher view you can take to bring some perspective to your problems.

GET INTO YOUR FLOW

You know that feeling you get when you're doing something challenging and enjoyable? The feeling of being so deeply involved in something that you lose all track of time? That feeling is called flow, and it can be a huge contributor to your well-being.

Psychologist Mihaly Csikszentmihalyi was the first to describe the experience of flow in psychological terms. He discovered that the circumstances most conducive to entering into flow are when both your skill level and the challenge before you are high and roughly evenly matched.

Frequently experiencing flow guarantees at least a minimum level of well-being, and for many people, it can be the experience that takes them from "My life is good" to "My life is great!"

For this exercise, all you need to do is engage in an activity that is both challenging and enjoyable, one that requires pushing yourself beyond your comfort zone to complete.

Are you a programmer who is passionate about your work? Set yourself a coding challenge and create something you never have before.

Do you love competitive gaming? Enter a competition and pit your skills against the best in the business.

Making flow a regular part of your life will boost your well-being and will benefit you in many other areas such as skill building and self-development.

COMMIT TO YOUR CURRENT ACTIVITY

This will not be the easiest exercise to improve your well-being, but it's one that can have far-reaching impacts on your life. Depending on what you are doing, it can take just a bit of extra effort, or it can be a huge challenge!

This exercise is called "Commit to Your Current Activity," and the name speaks for itself—to engage in this exercise all you need to do is fully commit to whatever you are currently doing.

* If you're at work, slogging through a particularly tedious task, dedicate yourself to doing it right and doing it well.
* If you're at home, up to your elbows in dirty dishes and suds, apply yourself to becoming the most effective dishwasher there ever was.
* If you're reading a bedtime story to your child, focus all of your energy on giving a great performance. Imagine your role is up for an Oscar, and do whatever it takes to win!

Committing fully to an activity is an excellent tool for keeping yourself in the moment and ensuring that you are living your life, or at least this little piece of your life, to the best of your abilities.

Pouring all of your energy into a task you don't enjoy can be difficult, but on the plus side, you will probably get it done faster!

CHAPTER 2

EXERCISES TO INCREASE POSITIVE EMOTIONS

Positive emotions, such as joy, inspiration, and happiness, are the spices that add flavor to the dish that is your life. They may not make the bulk of your meal (those are the more substantial components of well-being, meaning, and healthy relationships), but they are what take your dish from plain and nutritious to exciting and delicious. You can't make a meal of only spices—imagine the satisfaction you would get from a mouthful of salt and pepper or lemon and dill—but they act as accents to the base ingredients.

This is similar to how positive emotions enhance and improve your life; you can't have a great life with positive emotions alone, but adding a dash or two to an already full life can help you get from good to great. Try these exercises to add flavor and good feelings to your life.

PRACTICE 2-MINUTE KINDNESS

One of the quickest and easiest ways to provide yourself with a boost of good feelings is to do something kind for someone else. Although humans have the potential to be quite nasty to one another, the urge to act kindly is also a strong one, and it can have lasting effects.

At some point in your day, take a 2-minute break to do something kind for someone else. You can do anything you'd like, as long as it is kind and it takes no more than 2 minutes (you can stretch this rule later, but try to start out with small, time-restricted acts).

If you're not sure where to start with your 2-minute kindness, consider trying one of these example acts:

1. Take 2 minutes to write a short email or text message praising a coworker or complimenting a friend.
2. Strike up a quick, casual conversation with the shy new person at school or in the office while you're on your way to your next class or meeting.
3. If you see someone drop their groceries or their mail, stop and take a minute or two to help them pick everything up and put everything back in order.

If none of these examples sound relevant to you, choose whatever act of kindness comes naturally to you. Using just 2 minutes of your day to do something kind for others will have a much larger impact on your happiness than you can imagine.

COUNT YOUR KINDNESSES

You know that little rush of good feeling you get when you do something nice for another person? This exercise will allow you to remember and relive that feeling!

This exercise has two parts:

1. Do at least two or three random acts of kindness each day. For example, you could leave an extra-large tip for your barista, hold the door for someone in a hurry, or give a coworker a heartfelt compliment.
2. Write down your kind acts in a journal or notebook at the end of the day.

Writing down things that you are grateful for is a popular practice, and that's a great exercise too. However, this exercise focuses on improving your happiness and positive emotions instead of targeting gratitude alone.

Simply engaging in the first step will boost your mood, but looking back on your kind acts at the end of the day will allow you to recapture and relive that good feeling. If you have many acts of kindness to write down at the end of the day, you'll multiply the good feeling and have several acts to point to when you start feeling down about yourself.

Try to do this activity every day if you can; however, if you forget to keep track of your kind acts on a particular day, at least take a few moments before bed to look over the kind things you did in the last few days.

TREAT THIS DAY AS IF IT WERE YOUR LAST DAY

How often do you notice your mood getting worse because of little things, like traffic or a minor disagreement with your significant other? It probably happens more often than you'd like. It's surprisingly easy to let little things drag you down. Luckily, it's also fairly easy to put them in perspective.

This exercise is based on a pretty popular idea of shifting your perspective from the small and ultimately insignificant things to the broader picture.

When you find yourself bogged down in all the little things that have gone wrong in your day, stop and ask yourself two questions:

1. What if today were the last day of my life?
2. How would I want to spend my day if it were my last?

These two simple questions have the extraordinary power to pull you out of your temporary bad mood and take you to the 30,000-foot view of your life. From this perspective, even the things that made you most angry or irritated during the day become no bigger than specks, not even worth mentioning. However, the truly good things will remain as big as ever.

Imagining today as your last day will help you to put aside minor annoyances and focus on the positive things you value most.

THINK OF THREE FUNNY THINGS

This exercise involves identifying funny things you experienced over the course of your day. You've probably heard it said that laughter is the best medicine; the jury is still out on how true this is, but we know that laughter is an excellent way to boost your mood!

During your daily routine, pay attention to what makes you smile. Take special note of anything that makes you laugh. If something makes you burst into uncontrollable laughter, write yourself a note to be sure you remember it later.

At the end of your day, take out your trusty journal, and make an entry titled "Three Funny Things."

1. Write down three funny things you remember from your day. For example, you might write something like:

   * My coworker accidentally drank my tea instead of his coffee and made a funny face.
   * My friend told me that funny joke about dogs at lunch, and I snorted into my drink.
   * On my way home, I saw a man dressed in a silly costume doing an energetic dance on the street.

2. Remember how funny it was when you heard or saw these things earlier in your day, and allow yourself to laugh all over again.

Completing this exercise will help you to see the funnier side of life, and go to bed with a smile on your face.

SOLVE A PROBLEM WITH HUMOR (HYPOTHETICALLY)

This is another exercise that focuses on humor to help you feel good. However, instead of simply noting the funny things that happened to you during your day, you get a chance to flex your creative muscles and come up with some funny scenarios of your own.

1. Think about something stressful or upsetting that happened to you today. It doesn't need to be a tiny annoyance, but you should avoid picking something overly serious (e.g., think about stepping in a puddle and soaking your shoes versus a heated argument with your spouse).
2. Write a sentence or two about this problem, or just come up with a good explanation of it in your head.
3. Next, come up with a funny way that it could have been resolved. The sky is the limit here, so don't be afraid to think outside the box!

For example, if your problem was stepping in a puddle and soaking your shoes, a funny way for the problem to be resolved could be a man rushing over to you and stopping you right before you planted your foot in the puddle, then proclaiming himself the superhero of dry feet and "flying" off down the street, a clenched fist extending before him and an imaginary cape swirling behind him.

Whatever you write, make sure it tickles your funny bone! Practicing this exercise regularly will teach you to be creative when solving your problems and will help you see the humor in everyday life.

SAVOR SOMETHING GOOD

The practice of savoring is an easy and effective way to increase positive emotions. Savoring refers to directing all of your attention toward something you are experiencing with one (or more) of your senses, including taste, smell, sound, or touch. To savor is to truly taste every component of your food, to appreciate every note of the song you are listening to, or to smell a good scent and allow your brain to make the natural connections between smell and memory.

You can choose to savor something more complicated than a single-sense activity, such as one that involves multiple movements or steps, but it is easier to begin with something simple.

If you've never tried savoring before, it is best to begin with food. Grab something you like to eat or something that you're excited to try, and go to a quiet place where you can sit uninterrupted.

Take a moment or two to just smell the food before taking a bite. Hold that first bite in your mouth for a moment, feeling the texture and the temperature, noting all the tastes that combine to make the food. Chew slowly and mindfully before swallowing, then note whether there is a lingering taste in your mouth once the food is gone.

Eat the rest of your food in this manner, savoring every bite. Once you have mastered savoring food, challenge yourself to savor more complicated things, like taking a walk or doing laundry.

CREATE A BALANCING ACT

This exercise is based on the idea that balance is where happiness can be found. We all have to do things we don't want to in our lives, but that doesn't mean you simply throw up your hands and give in; there are some things you may be able to craft, change, or alter to make those things more palatable to you.

Get out your journal or a piece of notebook paper and draw two columns. Label column one "Things I Like to Do," and label column two "Things I Have to Do."

Under column one, list things that are not essential for your day-to-day survival but which help you live a happy and fulfilling life. For example, you would not write "eating" here, but you might write "indulging in an occasional happy hour snack."

Under column two, list the things that *are* essential for you to function as an independent adult. You might write things like "going to work" or "getting my oil changed" in this column.

Compare the two columns and ask yourself these questions:

* Which things in column one are especially good for my well-being?
* Which things in column two do I particularly dislike doing?

Try to come up with ways to combine these two sets of activities into your daily routine, especially those that you don't generally enjoy. For instance, if listening to music is in column one and vacuuming is in column two, try vacuuming with your headphones on next time.

TURN ON YOUR POSITIVE FILTER

This exercise is one of those that is much harder to practice than it is to preach. It might not seem so hard to give this exercise a try, but making it a regular practice is where it gets difficult; however, as challenging as it may be to put into practice, it's not impossible!

Positive filtering is changing your perspective on the things you see around you. You must let in at least some of the negative things around you for safety and health reasons, but many of us get overwhelmed with the negative and forget to let the positive in as well.

To turn on your positive filter, stop whatever you are doing and take a good look around you. Notice at least one positive thing, like the cheerful sunshine, the leaves blowing in the breeze, a smiling mother and child walking down the street, or a picture of your children on the desk in front of you.

If you truly can't find anything positive in your immediate vicinity, put the exercise on pause and try it again in a little while. Eventually you will be able to find *something* positive nearby.

That's it—that's the whole exercise! Of course, doing this just once won't help you build a more positive outlook—you must repeat this practice multiple times a day to cultivate your positive filter and open yourself up to all the good that life has to offer.

WRITE IN YOUR FUTURE DIARY

In times of doubt, disappointment, or pessimism, it can often be helpful to envision a positive future. In addition to soothing your fears and helping you open yourself up to possibility, this can be a great way to encourage yourself to strive toward a challenging goal. If you don't have a specific goal in mind at the moment, focus on a future in which you have found solutions to your biggest current problems.

Follow these steps to write your future diary entry:

1. Grab your journal, notebook, or diary (or even just a scrap of paper), and something to write with.
2. Give your entry a date that represents when you believe your goal may be accomplished or near completion.
3. Imagine yourself at this date and reflect on how you will feel. Consider how your life—including your work, relationships, and overall lifestyle—will have changed between now and then.
4. Write your diary entry for this future date, focusing on the progress you made to get there and the ways your life has improved since the present.

Visualizing a positive future in which you are nearing your goals or enjoying the fruits of your labor can boost your motivation, your optimism and self-confidence, and your current happiness.

RELAX!

You probably already know that stress can have a big impact on your mood. Addressing the major sources of stress in your life is a great way to improve your overall mood, but sometimes the sources of your stress are vague or out of your control.

In those cases, the best way to address your stress and improve your mood is to focus on what you *can* control: you!

Relaxation exercises are a great way to deal with stress and get an instant mood boost. This breathing exercise will help you relax and unwind.

Follow these steps to relaxation:

1. Sit in a comfortable position with your hands on your thighs, and close your eyes.
2. Take in one large breath through your nose, drawing out the inhale to 5 seconds.
3. Hold the breath in your lungs for another 5 seconds.
4. Steadily release your breath out through your mouth, drawing out the exhale to 5 seconds once again.
5. Be still and don't take in another breath for 5 seconds.
6. Repeat these steps for at least 3 minutes or until you are calmer and more relaxed.

If you don't have the best lung capacity, try changing each breathing step to 3 seconds and slowly working your way up to 5 seconds. You'll get there with practice!

TALK ABOUT YOUR PROBLEMS

Paradoxically, talking about your problems can actually boost your happiness. Anyone who has had a good therapist can attest to this phenomenon; sometimes you spend the entire session talking about really difficult stuff, but you leave feeling much better than when you came in.

This happiness boost comes from the cathartic experience of getting something difficult or damaging off your chest. You may also benefit from the commiseration, advice, or perspective of the person you are speaking with.

So often, we get caught up in our own lives and forget that there are billions of other humans out there who have many of the same problems we have. Talking to someone who can identify with the problems you are having can be a great source of relief, and even those with no relevant experience can offer soothing empathy.

If you are struggling to come up with someone to talk about your problems with, and seeing a therapist is not feasible at the moment, consider chatting with a total stranger. Be on the lookout—on the Internet or in person—for a friendly or easy-going individual, and offer that person a chance to talk out their problems if they are willing to listen to you do the same.

Pouring your heart out to a stranger can be amazingly therapeutic; after all, they have no preconceived notions or judgments about you, and they can approach your situation from a relatively neutral viewpoint. Don't underestimate the wisdom that you may find in a stranger's words!

DOUBLE THE GOOD

In this exercise, you will trick your brain into experiencing a positive event twice, doubling the impact of the event on your happiness and well-being.

Think about the most positive thing that has happened to you in the last 24 hours. It doesn't have to be something big, but the happier it made you feel, the better! It could be receiving a compliment from a loved one, participating in a fun activity, or learning something new.

Whatever you have in mind, consider every detail of your experience. It may help you to write these features down on a piece of paper or in your notebook. For example, if your positive experience was getting a heartwarming hug from your child, you might write:

* She smiled sweetly at me and told me she loved me.
* She leaned in for a hug and wrapped her little arms and sticky hands tight around my neck.
* I put my nose to her hair and breathed in that wonderful smell of soap, apples, baby powder, and Cheerios.
* She held on to me for a few seconds, then squeezed as tightly as she could.

Make sure to note any details related to the memory-rich senses of smell and taste.

By recalling this experience in detail, you are stimulating your brain into living this experience all over again, doubling the feel-good chemicals and cementing positive memories.

WORK UP A SWEAT

Don't worry, you don't need to *literally* work up a sweat for this exercise—all you need to do is get up and move!

The link between physical activity and happiness is well established. Most people know that exercise releases endorphins (feel-good chemicals) in the body. Still, it can be difficult to get motivated.

For this exercise, don't think of exercising as a way to improve your physical health or your outward appearance. Instead, think only about the impact exercise has on happiness. Don't worry if you can't commit to a 45-minute workout routine or to a 60-minute yoga class—just dedicate a few minutes to doing something active.

It could be a quick walk up and down the block. It could be 1 minute of jumping jacks. It could be doing a set of ten push-ups or holding Tree Pose for 1 minute on each leg.

It doesn't really matter what you do as long as it involves movement. The point isn't necessarily to burn calories or to improve your heart health, but to get your brain working more positively and efficiently.

The next time you are struggling with a depressing thought or feeling lazy, unfocused, or just plain down, try spending a minute or two doing something active. You might find that you enjoy the activity and want to continue doing it, or you might stop as soon as you can, but you will likely find that you got a little mood boost from your physical exertion.

TRY THE POSSIBILITY MIND-SET

Inspiration is a powerful motivator as well as a mood-enhancer—it can have a huge impact on how you feel!

For this exercise, you will put your negative thinking on pause and allow yourself to dwell only on the positive.

1. Think about a current problem or challenge in your life. Is there something that feels overwhelming or impossible?
2. Consider your current thoughts about this problem. They're probably along the lines of "There's no way I can..." or "It's too difficult to..."
3. Write down these negative or pessimistic thoughts on a piece of paper with some space on the page in between thoughts.
4. Now try the possibility mind-set: instead of focusing on all the obstacles between you and solving your problem or meeting your goal, think about all of the possibilities that this challenge opens up to you.
5. For each negative thought, run it through the possibility mind-set, and write down what comes out on the other side. For example, "There's no way I can figure this out" could become "I have what it takes to find the solution."
6. Do this for each negative thought. Once you have completed each pair, read through them and highlight, underline, or otherwise call attention to the positive thought. This will help you plant the new thought in your mind.

Revisit these positive thoughts whenever you need a little inspiration.

CHAPTER 3

EXERCISES TO BUILD RESILIENCE

In a perfect world, you would have no need of resilience. However, as you likely already know, you do not live in a perfect world! Even the happiest and luckiest people will suffer at some point. You will face disappointment, pain, and tragedy in your life, but you can choose how you respond. People who are resilient fall down just as much as the rest of us, but they always choose to get back up again.

This kind of resilience is a wonderful trait to have, and it is certainly worth the time and effort to develop. It will not only help you minimize the impact of life's stressors, it will also aid you in coming out of an ordeal stronger than you were when you went in. If you're ready to build up your ability to bounce back, give the exercises in this chapter a try.

USE POSITIVE REALISM

Unsurprisingly, people who are more optimistic tend to have greater resilience. When you expect good things to happen, it's not so hard to bounce back from the occasional obstacle or setback. It works in the other direction, too—when you're always bouncing back to new opportunities and picking up lessons learned along the way, it's easy to be optimistic about the future.

Because of this relationship between resilience and optimism, one of the best ways to improve one is to boost the other. There are many exercises on boosting your long-term optimism in Chapter 4, but try this quick exercise if your focus is ultimately on building resilience.

Positive realism is one type of optimism that is accessible even to those who are not natural optimists. The positive realist may acknowledge that the worst is possible, but they spend far more energy hoping and planning for the best.

Give this mind-set a try with the following steps:

1. Think of an upcoming event or occasion that you are worrying about.
2. Consider all the different possible outcomes (e.g., if the event is a date, think about all the different ways it could turn out, from falling madly in love to leaving in disgust).
3. Determine which outcomes are the most likely. Of these most likely outcomes, at least one or two will be positive (e.g., planning a second date, making a new friend).
4. Commit yourself to looking forward to these positive, realistic outcomes.

LOOK FOR THE SILVER LINING

One of the ways in which resilient people differ from the not-so-resilient is in their ability to see the positive in any situation, also known as finding the silver lining. Those high in resilience tend to search for the positive when they face a struggle rather than wallowing in the negative. To build your resilience, practice finding the silver lining.

The next time you are faced with a challenging, upsetting, or painful situation, find a quiet moment to sit and think. Come up with at least one positive outcome or side effect of your situation. It may take you a while, but don't give up! Something will eventually come to you.

The silver lining could be a new door of possibility opening up when a much-desired one closes. It could be that a positive thing happens to someone else as a result of your situation. If there is really no direct positive effect, then perhaps the silver lining is that you will come out the other side stronger and wiser.

Once you become adept at finding the silver lining, you can aim to come up with a balance of positive and negative effects instead of one solitary good thing. In other words, for every negative aspect of a situation, you could acknowledge that it *is* painful or difficult—but note that something good comes out of it as well.

Practice finding the silver lining and you will find yourself well on the way to enhanced resilience!

OPEN YOURSELF UP TO KINDNESS

As you may have noticed from the many mentions of kindness so far, it is a vital piece of the puzzle of a good life. Those people who regularly engage in (and receive) acts of kindness seem to operate with a sort of internal store of good feelings and goodwill toward others.

Take advantage of the many benefits that kindness offers not only by engaging in acts of kindness yourself, but also by opening yourself up to acts of kindness directed toward you.

Each day, challenge yourself to engage in at least one act of kindness toward someone else, and identify at least one act of kindness in which you are on the receiving end.

You may find the first part to be much easier than the second; after all, you can control your own behavior, but you have no control over others' behavior! However, you will quickly find that people practice a million little acts of kindness every day. Did someone wave you in ahead of them when you were desperately trying to get in the turn lane? There's an act of kindness! Did someone hold the elevator door for you instead of hitting the close button when they saw you coming? There's another kind act!

You are truly surrounded by kindness each and every day. Taking note of this kindness and drinking it in will allow you to build up a store of positivity that you can turn to when you face tragedy or trauma.

FACE YOUR FEARS

This exercise might be one of the most difficult in this book, depending on your fears. It's intimidating to seek out that which scares you the most and confront it, but there is no feeling like successfully emerging on the other side of the confrontation.

Facing your fears teaches you that you have deeper reserves of courage, fortitude, and strength than you know. It sheds light on just how tough and brave you can be, and it gives you a boost of confidence and resilience that you can carry with you for life.

The first step to facing your fears is, of course, identifying your greatest fears. If you have a greater than normal fear response or a phobia, you should seek the advice and guidance of a professional before trying to face your fear on your own. However, if you are struggling with a less pathological fear, give yourself a chance to tackle it on your own.

Once you've identified your fear, find some way to bring yourself face to face with it in a safe, controlled environment. For example, if you are afraid of spiders, set up some time with a knowledgeable tarantula owner or spider expert to handle a spider. If you are scared of public speaking, sign up for a group like Toastmasters that offers people from all levels of experience a chance to practice and forbids any bad audience behavior.

Facing your fears and living to tell the tale will provide an excellent boost for your confidence and resilience.

GET OUTDOORS

Getting outside is good for you in so many ways. When you venture out, you get some fresh air, move your body, enjoy a change of scenery, and appreciate nature.

Getting outdoors has another potential benefit you may not know: it helps you boost your resilience.

While you enjoy the sunshine and cool breeze, you are also opening yourself up to new ways of thinking. Just being outside can broaden your perspective and help you see past what's immediately in front of you. Strolling through nature encourages you to think outside the box and open your mind to all the possibility the world has to offer.

To take advantage of this nature boost, all you need to do is go outside!

Sometime during your busy day, make the time to spend at least a few minutes outside. Take a walk in the woods, jog on the beach, hike up to a waterfall, or simply stand outside and feel the sunshine on your face. When you come back inside, it might help to journal about your experience or to revisit the problem or issue you were thinking about before you went out. You may find that the problem is a little easier to solve than it was earlier!

If you find it difficult to get out every day, at least keep this suggestion in mind and put it to the test next time you are feeling upset, anxious, or sad.

DOCUMENT LESSONS LEARNED

We have all suffered from setbacks but, if you're reading this, you're still here! That means that you have recovered from past bumps in the road. Figuring out the tools you used to do this will help you improve your ability to rebound in the future.

To figure out how you survived and thrived through your troubles in the past, you need to conduct an investigation into your "lessons learned." In a business context, this term usually refers to a post-project-completion review or reflection on what worked well, what didn't, and what you learned about how to make future projects run smoother.

For your resilience lessons learned, you will consider the same aspects, except in the context of your personal development. Follow these steps to conduct a "lessons learned" reflection:

1. Think about one of the most difficult setbacks or failures you have experienced. Describe it in detail.
2. Reflect on how you made it through; ask yourself:

    * What helped me get through?
    * What did I do that made the situation more difficult?
    * If I faced a similar situation, what would I do the same and what would I do differently?

3. Wrap it all up in a set of bullet points on how you can successfully make it through any difficult situation.

Refer to these bullet points to identify your best strategies for bouncing back.

TAKE A MENTAL BREAK

This exercise may end up being your favorite—all it requires is to give yourself a break! Think about how you improve your physical strength. You need to work at it, completing regular exercises and ensuring that you get enough protein to build healthy muscles; however, it is also vital to let your body rest. If you do the same rigorous exercises over and over without allowing your muscles a chance to recover, you won't get much stronger.

If you want to improve your resilience, you also need to work at it. You need to put in time and effort to build up your "resilience muscles," but you also need to let them rest once in a while.

At least a few times a day, simply sit back and let your mind wander. You can daydream, fantasize, meditate, engage in a freestyle kind of prayer or reflection, or just think about nothing. Surprisingly, your brain can get a lot done when you don't provide it with any specific direction!

Taking a mental break helps your brain to piece together your experiences and memories from the day and make new connections, improving your problem-solving and decision-making abilities.

BOOST YOUR PROBLEM-SOLVING SKILLS

Many people tend to get overwhelmed when a particularly troublesome problem arises. When there is no clear-cut answer, it's easy to feel lost and begin to lose your confidence in your own abilities. This is a natural reaction, but it's not very good for your personal development or sense of resilience.

Next time you come up against a new problem, instead of just throwing up your hands in defeat, use this opportunity to develop your problem-solving skills.

List three to five ways you can potentially solve this new problem. Don't worry about coming up with the very best ways to solve the problem, just get some ideas out and on paper!

Once you have a good list, go through your options and come up with a couple of advantages and risks for each one. For example, if your problem is "my new coworker and I don't click," you might come up with the potential solution "avoid her whenever you can." This solution's advantages include being easy to do and minimizing the awkwardness of talking to her, but you also risk missing out on a good working relationship or seeming cold and unfriendly.

Do this for each potential solution, then rank them from most promising to least promising. You don't necessarily need to pick the top solution and run with it, but it should be one you would consider.

Practicing this exercise regularly will help you build more effective and creative problem-solving skills.

CREATE STEPS TO A SOLUTION

After coming up with potential solutions in the last exercise, you can practice coming up with small steps to carry you through the solution you choose to go with.

Some problems may feel so big that you don't see how you could possibly overcome them. When you are faced with such a problem, one of the best ways to keep yourself upright and moving forward is to break things down into small, meaningful steps.

Take one of the top solutions you came up with in the last exercise and think about what you would need to do to implement it. If you had to break your solution into parts, what would the first part be?

As an example, imagine your problem is a looming project deadline at work, and you've been procrastinating. The first part of your solution might be putting together an executive summary of your project.

Next is the most important piece—break that part into small, manageable steps. Your first step might be as simple as gathering all your project-related documents. Step two could be to open a blank document and give it a relevant title. In step three, you might create a high-level outline for the summary. Continue until you reach the end of your solution.

When you have all of your steps planned, the problem likely won't seem quite so large anymore. Practice stepping through your problems to build inner resilience and face your future challenges with greater confidence in your ability to overcome!

IDENTIFY YOUR GOALS

Having a set of goals that are achievable and meaningful to you can help carry you through the tough times. It's easier to persevere and bounce back when you have a desirable goal to motivate you!

You probably already know the benefits of having smart professional goals, but it can be difficult to come up with your own personal, meaningful goals.

If you've struggled to identify your goals, try these steps:

1. Identify what is most important to you. Think about what your values are, what your desires for your future are, and what makes you happiest. Write these things down in a notebook or journal.
2. Narrow this list to the most important three or four things. If you need help narrowing down, think about which things you feel you can't live without.
3. For each important thing, imagine what your life would look like if you put this front and center. Write a few sentences about how you'd like to incorporate or live out this value in your life.
4. Read over what you wrote for each important thing and distill the paragraph into a one-sentence goal with a specific, achievable outcome.

Congratulations, you've identified your life goals! However, your goals can shift as quickly as your interests, so do this exercise regularly for best results.

CHECK IN WITH YOUR GOALS

Once you have a set of life goals that you are excited to work toward, it will be easier to stay focused and motivated, even when trouble arises. When trouble does pop up, your goals will give you a great foundation for keeping yourself balanced and powering through.

Whenever you are struggling with something really stressful, do this quick exercise to keep your focus on what is most important and avoid getting stuck or stalled.

1. Press pause. Do a quick mindfulness exercise, meditate, or just breathe for a few moments to clear your head.
2. Think about your goals. Write them down or pull out your journal or notebook to remind yourself of your goals.
3. Ask yourself whether you are making progress and working toward your goals right now. If you're not on track, think about how you got sidetracked.
4. Identify the quickest way to get from where you are currently to where you need to be in order to eventually achieve your goals.
5. Put your plan into action!

This is one of the best ways to boost your resilience because it builds on your existing motivation to meet your goals and gives you multiple opportunities to rededicate yourself to achieving them.

MIND YOUR PPPS (PERMANENCE, PERVASIVENESS, AND PERSONALIZATION)

This exercise can help you build resilience, boost your optimism, and exert more control over your own life.

We all deal with negative thoughts from time to time; however, sometimes we don't even recognize negative thoughts for what they are. Follow these steps to identify and challenge those thoughts that are holding you back from being happy, healthy, and resilient.

First, learn about the PPPs, three traits that can keep you feeling unhappy and thinking negatively:

* **Permanence** encourages people to expect bad times or bad events to last forever.
* **Pervasiveness** refers to letting something bad in one area of life poison all other areas of life.
* **Personalization** is what people do when they blame themselves for anything bad that happens.

Then scan your thoughts for PPPs and try this:

1. When one of your thoughts contains any of these negative characteristics, write the thought down.
2. Figure out which PPP category it falls into and write that down too.
3. Come up with an alternate thought. For example, replace "I'm never going to feel better" with "I feel horrible right now, but it will pass."
4. Read or repeat these alternate thoughts aloud regularly.

DO THE OPPOSITE

People high in resilience generally don't waste much time dwelling on their sorrows. When they get knocked down, they might take some time to gather their thoughts and engage in some vital self-care, but before long they're getting back on their feet and deciding on their next move.

People who aren't high in resilience tend to do the opposite; when they get knocked down, they stay where they are or even take a few steps back.

Although this is an understandable urge, it usually isn't as effective as the methods of resilient people. To build up your resilience, try adopting some of their ways.

One way to do this is to do the opposite—meaning, do the opposite of what you would usually do!

If you usually go home and wrap yourself in a blanket when you face disappointment, try going out for dinner or drinks with friends instead.

If your first instinct is to quit something when you run into a particularly difficult situation, try sticking it out and doubling down on your commitment.

If your go-to coping method is indulging in junk food, look up some new healthy recipes and get cooking!

Your feelings have a strong influence over your actions, but they don't have to decide your actions for you. By doing the opposite of whatever you feel like doing when faced with failure or disappointment, you are training yourself to make better decisions whether you feel like it or not.

ACCEPT THE CHANGE

You have probably heard the phrase "Nothing is certain but death and taxes." While it skews the taxman's eagerness to collect his due, it also highlights a fundamental truth of life: life is change, and changing is living.

Humans are in a constant state of flux; to stop changing would be to stop living. It's ironic and unfortunate that many people fear change, given this fundamental truth!

Luckily, this fear of change is not a permanent trait. You can work to overcome it. You may not learn to love change, but you can learn to accept it as an unavoidable part of life, and in the process, build your resilience.

To practice acceptance of change, write down these statements and keep them nearby (perhaps in your wallet or as a digital note on your phone):

* Change is inevitable.
* Change is a sign that you are growing.
* Change is a sign that you are learning.
* Change is a chance to discover exciting new things about yourself and the world around you.
* Remember your darkest moment—without change, you would still be there.
* Remember your brightest moment—with change, you might revisit that moment in the future.

Whenever you find yourself dreading an upcoming change, read these statements to yourself.

CHAPTER 4

EXERCISES TO IMPROVE OPTIMISM

By now you've certainly heard about the many benefits of optimism. Compared with pessimists, optimists do better in school, have more success at work, excel in their hobbies, and may even live longer, healthier lives. With all of these positive outcomes, it's certainly worth a try to inject a little more optimism into your life!

You might be thinking that you'd like to be more optimistic, but that pessimism and optimism seem like pretty stable traits that are basically fixed once you reach adulthood. It's true that pessimism and optimism are on the more stable side of the various aspects of personality, but they are certainly not set in stone. It takes time and effort, but with regular practice, you can boost your optimism and get better at seeing the brighter side of things.

VISUALIZE A POSITIVE POTENTIAL VERSION OF YOUR FUTURE SELF

This exercise works by helping you visualize one of your many positive potential futures. Allowing yourself to believe in a positive future is a fundamental piece of being optimistic, and visualizing a positive and realistic version of yourself can help you get there.

Take some time to think about the goals you have set for your life that are most important to you. Consider how likely it is for you to reach all of these goals within one lifetime. Which goals are compatible with one another? Are any goals incompatible? What goals would you be willing to sacrifice if it meant you could meet other goals?

From your answers to these questions, build a mental image of what this future will look like and how it will feel to have met the goals you identified as most important. Gather as much detail as you can: who you are with, what you are doing, where you are living, and how you are feeling. Think about whether you would feel regret over not meeting each of the goals you originally set for yourself, or whether you would feel satisfied and fulfilled focusing on the goals you *have* met.

This exercise can be especially helpful when you are feeling overwhelmed by all of your goals, since it reminds you that it's okay to let some things go—you can still be a happy and fulfilled person, even if you don't meet each and every goal you set for yourself!

KEEP A POSITIVE DIARY

Journaling is a great practice for many reasons: it can help you make sense of jumbled thoughts, it can help you work through your emotions, and it can facilitate self-reflection. Including both positive and negative experiences in your entries is important for authenticity.

However, if you're looking to boost your optimism, you might want to try keeping a positive diary. As the name implies, this is a diary in which you focus on the positive experiences you have. If you wish to journal for the standard reasons, feel free to keep a comprehensive journal and a positive journal as well.

Each night, just before bed, take out your positive journal and go over your day, scanning for the good things that happened. These can include good things that happened to you, good things that you witnessed happening to others, or even good things you did for yourself or for others. Basically, if it happened in the last day and it can be described as positive, write it down!

If you had a particularly excellent meal, write it down. If you saw a romantic public proposal, write it down. If you offered your assistance to a friend in need, write it down. You get the picture—if it was good, write it down!

Each day, you will create a list of new reasons to smile and be optimistic. This is an excellent way to make sure you end your day on a positive note.

FAKE IT 'TIL YOU MAKE IT

You probably heard this phrase from a parent or teacher at some point, as encouragement for doing something you were anxious or insecure about doing. They probably told you that most people don't know what they're doing, but they figure it out as they go.

Well, as you've surely noticed in your own life, they were right! Many of us try new things with no prior knowledge or experience, and just figure it out while doing it. Lots of people take new positions they don't feel ready for, but apply themselves to learning on the job.

"Faking it 'til you make it" is a surprisingly common learning technique, and it is one that works for learning optimism as well. If you feel like there's no way you could just try a couple of exercises and become a positive thinker, this method may be for you.

Instead of trying to force yourself to think positively, try simply *acting* like you're thinking positively. Even if you're predicting doom and gloom on the inside, do what an optimist would do. Think about what a person expecting a positive outcome would do and commit to taking the same actions. After all, your thoughts don't need to match your actions. You don't have to be expecting the worst to prepare for it, and you don't need to feel particularly cheery to plan for the best.

Eventually, that positive outer attitude will begin to seep in, creating a positive inner attitude as well.

FOCUS ON THE PRESENT

Optimists tend to not dwell too much on the past or get lost in thoughts of the future, but live fully in the present. When you fully engage with the present, you open yourself up to all the good things happening around you. Instead of lamenting something that happened to you in the past, you could be actively contributing to a positive present.

Follow these steps to turn your focus from the past or future to the present:

1. Check in regularly with your thoughts. Pause wherever you are and whatever you're doing, and scan your thoughts for preoccupation with the past or future.
2. When you've caught yourself in the act, identify the thought and write it down or make a mental note of it.
3. Think about how this thought ties in to your current goals, and identify the most relevant goal. Come up with one idea or action you can take right now or in the very near future to move yourself closer to this goal.

For example, if you find yourself thinking about the time you missed an important deadline, you might tie it to your goal of avoiding procrastination. Instead of dwelling on your past misstep, come up with a step you can take today to break yourself of your procrastination habit, such as taking one concrete action on the project with the nearest deadline.

Give yourself reasons to be optimistic, and you'll find it much easier to actually *be* optimistic!

WATCH YOUR LANGUAGE

No, the title of this exercise doesn't refer to swearing! It concerns the negative language people use on themselves. This negative language is demoralizing, and it can also hold you back from being your best self.

This exercise will help you to be more aware of the negative language you use with yourself and come up with alternative language to replace those unhelpful thoughts.

Follow these three simple steps:

1. Start checking in regularly with your thoughts. Train yourself to pause your train of thought at least a few times a day and scan for any negative language you are using with yourself.
2. Identify the negative language. You will quickly learn which words and phrases you use the most often. For example, you may frequently catch yourself saying, "There's no way that I can…" or "I always screw up when…"
3. Replace the negative language. Instead of thinking to yourself, "There's no way that I can…," try "It might work out…" And instead of thinking, "I always screw up when…," replace the thought with "I usually succeed when…"

Replacing the negative language with more helpful, optimistic language will help you develop a new tendency to look on the bright side.

REFRAME YOUR NARRATIVE

Your narrative is the story of what made you who you are today. It's your biography, with your current self as the ending. Putting together a narrative requires self-reflection and consideration of what forces in your past shaped you to become the person you are now.

However, you can't create one narrative and expect it to fit for years to come; you are always changing and shifting from one version of yourself to the next. As you change, the most significant aspects of your narrative change as well; new experiences are added, and early experiences are added or dropped as their influence on your current self changes.

Since your story is ever changing, this presents you with a great opportunity to purposely shape your narrative. You can use the narrative in the opposite direction—reimagining your current self by reimagining your narrative.

If you don't already have an articulated narrative, whether in your mind or on paper, take some time to put one together.

Think about your most negative life experiences. No doubt they helped shape who you are today, but they may have had an overly negative impact.

For each experience, shift your focus from the negative ways it impacted you and focus instead on what you gained. What did you learn from the experience? How did it help you grow?

Rewrite relevant portions of your narrative with the positive outcomes highlighted, and consider how this results in a more positive and optimistic version of your current self.

MANAGE YOUR EXPECTATIONS

The biggest culprit behind your tendency to be negative may be faulty or skewed expectations. It's difficult to be positive if things never turn out how you expect them to!

For this reason, it's important that you manage your expectations and set realistic goals. If you expect excessively positive outcomes, or positive outcomes in an extremely short period of time, you are setting yourself up for disappointment.

To avoid this disappointment, manage your expectations with the following steps:

1. Think about what you are hoping to achieve, and describe your time frame and desired outcome in detail.
2. Consider whether this outcome is realistic for the average person. Would the average person plucked off the street be able to meet this goal, if motivated to do so?
3. Consider how much sacrifice this outcome will require. For example, can you give up a little bit of time each day or several hours on the weekend and meet your goal? Or would achieving the goal require several hours a day?
4. Think about whether achieving your desired goal will truly lead to the outcome you expect. If your goal is specific to one area of life, such as your work, are you expecting it to also have a large, positive impact on other areas of your life?

This exercise might seem like a buzzkill, but it's vital to have realistic expectations if you hope to maintain your optimism.

PRACTICE FORGIVENESS

One of the best things you can do for your own sense of optimism is to let go of old disappointments and grudges. Extending forgiveness to those people who have wronged you is not really a generous act for them, it's a generous act for yourself!

Instead of carrying around all the wrongs done to you as emotional baggage, try forgiving the transgressors and letting the hurt go.

To practice this liberating and uplifting exercise, first identify an old wound you are still nursing. Note what happened, who wronged you, and what the fallout over the incident was. Accept that these are the facts, and that nothing can change them.

Next, think about how the experience changed you. It may have made you more cautious and less willing to be vulnerable, but it may have also taught you something important about yourself and your needs and values. Note any positive growth that occurred.

Think about the person who hurt you. Remind yourself that he or she is human, and therefore makes mistakes, just like you and those you love. Imagine yourself in their shoes and come up with a scenario in which you may have taken the same action.

Write your words of forgiveness down or say them out loud: "[Person's name], I forgive you for [the wrong]."

This exercise will help you identify a grudge, acknowledge any good that came of it, empathize with the other person, and put the hurt behind you.

CELEBRATE THE SUCCESS OF OTHERS

Aside from improving your relationships with others, being positive and congratulatory when someone else succeeds benefits you as well. When you spend time cultivating an orientation to success and an attitude of appreciating success, no matter who it is that's enjoying that success, you will find that success comes more easily to you too.

The next time you are feeling down about or wallowing in envy of another's success, try this technique to bring yourself out of your funk and encourage yourself to think optimistically:

1. Think about how much time and effort that person put into her success. Generally, achievements and accolades don't just fall into your lap—you have to work for them.
2. Next, imagine how this person is feeling about her success. Visualize her sense of joy, accomplishment, and pride.
3. Put yourself in her shoes. Imagine you are experiencing this success, and open yourself up to the same feelings of joy, accomplishment, and pride. Revel in this feeling of success.
4. Remind yourself that her success is not related to yours. Her success doesn't make your future success any less likely.
5. Wrap all of these thoughts and feelings up into a sense of pride and happiness for the other person. Commit to congratulate her and to mean it when you say it.

DO ONE THING DIFFERENTLY

Sometimes all it takes to look on the bright side is changing one single action. When you feel overwhelmed or bogged down with a problem, it can paralyze you with fear of doing the wrong thing or confusion about what the right thing is.

In one of these times, deciding on a course of action and taking just one step toward that course can have a huge impact on how you feel. It can break the paralysis and remind you that you are capable of handling whatever you are dealing with.

Practice this technique of doing one thing differently, and you will develop a more positive view of yourself and of your ability to handle any problems that you face.

The next time you are struggling with this kind of situation, ask yourself one important question: "What one thing could I do differently to improve my situation?"

Come up with a few different options, and decide on which one is the best. It might be the easiest step you could take right now, or the one that will set you up for future steps. Whatever it is, take it and run with it!

Doing this exercise regularly when you run into a difficult situation will turn your focus from the problem to the potential solutions, shifting you into a more optimistic frame of mind.

ASK YOUR FUTURE SELF

It's easier to focus on the positive and let go of the negative when you have a coach, partner, or friend helping you along. Of course, you probably do not have constant access to a coach, partner, or friend (and you would likely get sick of each other quickly if you did)! You can't always turn to one of these people for an immediate pick-me-up, but you can create your own inner coach to help you stay motivated and optimistic.

Visualize your best future self (you can use the exercise "Visualize a Positive Potential Version of Your Future Self" in this chapter to prepare for this exercise). This future version of you has met all of his or her goals and has a positive outlook on life. Get to know this version of yourself, and spend some time understanding him or her front to back.

The next time you are struggling with deciding what to do next or having trouble looking on the bright side, ask your future self what he or she would do.

Based on what your future self has experienced and learned since the present, he or she will be able to provide you with a useful answer on what to do.

This might not feel as satisfying as talking directly with a loved one, but it will do in a pinch! As an added benefit, it will also help you figure out where you want to go and who you want to be in the future.

WEIGH THE EVIDENCE

If you're a realist, you probably struggle to embrace positive expectations, thinking that it doesn't make sense to always look on the bright side—you know that things can't always go your way and, at least some of the time, you will be disappointed.

It's true that sometimes you will be disappointed. However, it can be easy to overestimate the likelihood of negative outcomes and underestimate the likelihood of positive outcomes.

To correct this tendency, here's an exercise that realists should love. Follow these steps to give it a try:

1. The next time you find yourself expecting the worst, create a column in your notebook titled "Potential Outcomes" and write down all possible outcomes for the situation. Include both positive and negative outcomes.
2. Create a new column to the right, and title it "Evidence For." In this column, you will come up with evidence that each outcome will occur.
3. Create another column titled "Evidence Against." Here, list any reasons that each outcome will not occur.
4. Weigh the evidence! Think about both the evidence for and the evidence against each outcome, and decide how likely each outcome truly is.
5. Create one last column and use it to rank the likelihood of the possible outcomes.

This exercise will open your eyes to all of the ways that things can turn out positively.

COMPARE THE PROS AND CONS OF BEING POSITIVE

This exercise involves weighing the pros and cons of being positive and negative rather than the likelihood of certain outcomes.

Give this exercise a try when you are struggling between optimism and pessimism.

1. Describe the situation you are in that has you undecided. Make sure you understand what the potential outcomes are.
2. Next, identify the pros and cons of approaching the situation with optimism. Ask yourself how being optimistic would help you here, and whether it might set you up for unrealistic expectations.
3. When you have identified the pros and cons of optimism, do the same for pessimism. Ask yourself how expecting a negative outcome could help you here. Consider whether preparing for such an outcome would be more beneficial than expecting a positive outcome.
4. Compare your pros and cons, and see which option has more pros and which has more cons.

Occasionally, pessimism will have more pros than optimism, because sometimes preparing for the worst is the wisest thing to do. However, you will find that optimism is quite often the better choice.

TRY A MORNING VISUALIZATION

Get your day off to a good start with this exercise!

If you're like many people, your first thoughts in the morning are probably something like "It's already time to get up?" or "I have so many things I have to get done today," or even just "Ugh."

These thoughts are understandable, especially if you're not a morning person. However, they could be leading you to approach your day with a negative attitude. Starting the day off with a bad attitude can lead you to make bad decisions and pick out the negative in every situation instead of seeing the positive.

To avoid getting up on the wrong foot, so to speak, try this exercise.

First, you will need to identify your goals for the day and determine what it will take to meet them. When you've got a good idea of what meeting your goals will look like, you can begin the visualization piece.

Imagine that it is the end of the day and you have accomplished every goal you set for yourself today. Think about how it feels to have checked everything off your to-do list and to be that much closer to achieving your long-term goals.

Spend a few minutes noting as many details as possible about your near-future self. Really put yourself in his or her shoes and let yourself feel the sense of accomplishment after a day well spent.

Repeat each morning and watch as your newfound optimism helps you reach your goals.

CHAPTER 5

EXERCISES TO INCREASE GRATITUDE

Cultivating a sense of gratitude is all the rage these days. Everywhere you look, you'll see something about the benefits of gratitude. While gratitude is certainly a bit of a fad lately, it's with good reason. There truly are tons of benefits to being grateful, including being happier, being healthier, and enjoying better relationships.

Having gratitude doesn't mean you spend your whole day thanking people or engaging in grateful prayer or meditation; rather, having gratitude is more about your general attitude toward life. Being grateful helps you to appreciate all the good things in your life and cope with all the bad. It encourages you to be your best possible self and enjoy the life you have. Best of all, it doesn't take much to be grateful—just a few minutes a day can make all the difference. Use the exercises in this chapter to establish and maintain your gratitude practice.

FILL A GRATITUDE JAR

This is a simple exercise that will help you notice all the things you have to be grateful for, and you only need a few things to do it: a jar, some decorations (like glitter, ribbon, or stickers), a few sheets of colorful paper, and a pen.

Follow these steps:

1. Get a clear jar.
2. Decorate your jar however you'd like. You could paint the jar an attractive shade, thread a ribbon around it, cover it with stickers or glitter, or do anything else you'd like to make it something you like to look at.
3. Think of at least one or two things that happened throughout the day for which you are grateful. It can be something small, like getting a delicious sandwich for lunch, or something huge, like winning an award or landing your dream job. Cut up some strips of your colorful paper and write the things you are grateful for on them, then deposit them into the jar. Repeat this step throughout the day every day.

If practiced regularly, this exercise will result in a jar of countless things to be thankful for. It will help you realize what you love about your life and help you notice even more good things. If you are having a bad day and could use a quick mood booster, reach into the jar and grab a couple of random slips of paper. Read them to help yourself and acknowledge all the good things you have to be grateful for.

NOTE THREE GOOD THINGS

An old staple of the positive psychology and self-help movements, this exercise is a tried-and-true way of boosting your sense of gratitude.

As you go about your day, keep your eyes and ears peeled for any good things that happen to you. It can be all too easy to ignore all the positive things that happen and focus only on the negative things you encounter or experience, so it might take some practice—but don't give up!

At the end of the day, write down three good things that happened to you or around you on that day. They can be small things, like finding a ten-dollar bill in your pocket, or big things, like sharing a romantic new experience with your partner.

Once you have identified the three good things, take a few moments to think about why these things happened. Was it due to fate? Luck? Hard work? The kindness of a friend or family member? Write down two or three sentences on why each good thing happened to you.

Spending just a little bit of time at the end of your day to recognize the good in your life can remove the "negative events only" filter that may have taken residence in your mind and refocus your perspective to one of gratitude for the positive things you experience.

WRITE A GRATITUDE LETTER

This exercise requires only a piece of paper and a pen (a computer will also work). It's a simple exercise, but it can have a huge impact on your sense of gratitude and your happiness.

Begin by thinking about someone who did something good for you and who you have not actually thanked. This could be someone in your current life, like a friend or coworker, or it could be someone from your past, like a teacher or classmate. Whoever it is, make sure that they did something for which you are truly grateful and that you have not expressed your gratitude to them before.

Focusing on this act of generosity, sit down and write a letter to him or her. Remind this person what they did for you, and be as detailed and specific as you can (e.g., write "You gave me this specific advice..." rather than "You were always so helpful..."). Describe what this act meant to you at the time and what it means to you today. Tell him or her how it impacted your life and what you are doing now, if it is someone from your past.

Finally, thank this person sincerely for his or her action.

The end of this exercise is up to you—you can either keep this letter and consider writing the letter to be the whole point of the exercise, or you can actually send it out. Whichever ending you go with, you will enjoy an increase in gratitude.

PRACTICE A GRATITUDE MEDITATION

Standard meditation has the power to increase your gratitude and your well-being, but you can take the gratitude boost to the next level by focusing on being grateful *while* you meditate.

Start the way you would start a normal meditation session, sitting in a comfortable position in a quiet area. Shut down your eyes and begin to focus on your breathing.

Notice your breath as it comes in, filling your lungs, and as it goes out, rushing through your nostrils. Notice your belly as it rises and falls with each breath.

Once you have cleared your head, bring to mind something you are grateful for. It can be anything you are grateful for, but it's best if you think of something big, like your spouse, your health, or your home.

Focus on whatever you are grateful for and allow yourself to feel the full force of your gratitude. Let your gratitude flow through your body and fill you to the brim. Let it overflow. Let it pour out of you, and imagine it reaching all the way to the person or thing you are grateful for.

Spend a few minutes encouraging these feelings of gratitude, then allow yourself to float gently back to the present and go on with your day.

Practicing this meditation regularly will help you to enhance your sense of gratitude and encourage you to appreciate the good things in your life.

WALK WITH GRATITUDE

Walking itself is a great way to give your mood a temporary boost and to get your heart pumping. It's frequently prescribed for people new to fitness who want to adopt a healthier lifestyle, as it's gentle but effective. Taking a walk can also help you clear your mind, get some fresh air, and open up to greater creativity.

Now, take all of these benefits and top them off with a greater sense of gratitude. The gratitude walk is truly a multitasking exercise!

To turn any walk into a walk with gratitude, simply follow these steps:

1. Start off with your goal in mind: to be more grateful for all the good things in your life.
2. Clear your mind and allow yourself to take in every detail of the scenery around you. Whether you are walking in a busy city, down a sandy beach, or in serene woods, make sure you are actually seeing what is around you.
3. Appreciate the beauty of your surroundings. Even a busy city block has some beautiful things to look at, like two friends walking arm in arm, the blue sky peeking out around the buildings, and the birds chirping in the trees. Express your gratitude for seeing each lovely sight and hearing each pleasant sound, and even for smelling the energizing or mouthwatering scents of the city block.

The more you open yourself up to look for things to appreciate, the more things you will find to be grateful for.

CARRY A GRATITUDE TALISMAN

A talisman is an object that holds value and significance for the person who possesses it. It is a symbol of something important to them, and it can influence the person's actions and decisions by acting as a reminder of what they value. In more superstitious times, a talisman could also be something that had magical or supernatural powers to protect the possessor from evil or bring them luck.

You certainly don't have to ascribe any magical power to your gratitude talisman for this exercise to work—although you're free to do so if it matches your beliefs!

Pick an object that you think is pretty or striking. It should be small enough to fit in your pocket or purse, and it should feel pleasant to handle it (e.g., it is very smooth or has an interesting shape).

Carry this object with you throughout your day; take it with you when you go to work, to the grocery store, to run errands, or to pick the kids up from school or drop them off at soccer practice.

Whenever you happen to see the object, touch it, feel it shift, or pick it up, think of one thing you are grateful for. It doesn't need to be anything grand—it can be as small as feeling grateful for the ability to walk as you go about your errands.

At the end of the day, hold your gratitude talisman and think of all the things you had to be grateful for in your day.

COMPLETE THE PROMPTS

If you've never really practiced journaling before, you might be wondering where to begin. How do you get started? What do you actually write?

If this describes you, prompts might be just the thing you need! Prompts give you guidance and structure to help you get your creative juices flowing. After completing the prompts, you may find that you have some ideas about what to write after all.

To give prompts a try, write down the following in your journal:

* Five things I saw today that I am grateful for:
* Five things I heard today that I am grateful for:
* Five things I smelled today that I am grateful for:
* Five things I tasted today that I am grateful for:
* Five things I touched today that I am grateful for:
* Five people I am grateful for today:
* Five possessions I am grateful for today:
* Five things I usually take for granted that I am grateful for today:
* Five abilities I have that I am grateful for today:

If you have other ideas for prompts that you would enjoy completing, go ahead and add them to the list.

It's okay if you can't think of five things for each prompt every day. Just try to complete at least three or four of these prompts a day. Even if you only complete one or two, you will still end your day with more gratitude than before you wrote in your journal!

SAVOR YOUR MORNING COFFEE

Don't worry, if you don't drink coffee, you can use tea, juice, or any other food or drink you regularly consume in the morning! The coffee is not the important part of this exercise; starting your day with gratitude is what is important.

Whether you usually make a beeline to the coffeepot as soon as you wake or wait until you're heading out the door to pour your first cup, take a few extra minutes to sit and savor it before going on with your morning routine.

After you pour your cup and take a seat, direct your attention to all the pleasant things about your morning coffee. Before drinking, take a few moments to savor with your other senses.

* Notice the warmth of the cup in your hand. Wrap both hands around it and enjoy the sensation.
* Notice the aroma wafting out of the mug. Lower your head and breathe in the scent.
* Notice the sounds you are hearing, whether that's peaceful silence, chirping birds, or the sounds of your family getting ready for their day. Drink in the sounds and be grateful for what they represent.
* Notice the color of your coffee. Appreciate the deep, dark brown of black coffee or the creamy, smooth color of a latte.
* Finally, take a sip. Close your eyes and savor the taste.

If you have time, shift your focus to other things you have to be grateful for as you drink your coffee.

IMAGINE YOURSELF WITHOUT

This exercise may not be a great one for those feeling particularly stressed or depressed. It requires reflection on what life would be like without some of the things that make it worth living, which can be an upsetting exercise for some people. However, it can also be just what is needed to snap you out of a bad mood. Decide for yourself whether it's what you need right now or whether another exercise would be a better fit.

The next time you feel down, upset, disappointed, or simply lacking in gratitude, try this thought experiment.

Identify two or three things that make your life what it is today. These are things that you are most grateful for and which your life would be significantly different or more difficult without. For example, you may identify your job, your significant other, and your house or apartment.

Now, imagine that you don't have those things. Think about what your life would be like, right here and right now, without these things you are grateful for.

Without your job, you might not be able to support yourself or you might feel a lack of purpose.

Without your significant other, you wouldn't enjoy all of his or her little quirks and unique traits.

Without your home, you might be struggling to find a place to sleep.

Now imagine getting these things back one at a time, and allow yourself to experience a rush of gratitude for each thing.

CREATE A GRATITUDE INVENTORY

There's something so satisfying about making a list. If you are one of those people who find a surprising amount of enjoyment in making lists, you will love this exercise!

This exercise includes three steps:

1. Make a master list of things you are grateful for. Aim for fifty things if you are new to practicing gratitude, or one hundred if you feel grateful enough to come up with one hundred things!

2. Go through your list and notice the natural categories or groups. For example, you may notice that there are several family-oriented things, several work-related things, and many physical ability–related things. Take note of these natural categories.

3. Separate your list into the categories you identified. For example, gratitude for your spouse would go in the family category, gratitude for a new project at work would go into the work category, and gratitude for your ability to run would go in the physical ability category. Find the right category for each item on your list, even if this means making a new category or two as you go.

When you finish this exercise, you will have an inventory of fifty or one hundred reasons to be grateful for your life. Revisit this list whenever you are feeling ungrateful or unhappy with your life, and remind yourself of all the good things you have.

FLIP AN UNGRATEFUL THOUGHT

We all have ungrateful thoughts from time to time. Even the most grateful person on earth occasionally catches him- or herself thinking an ugly, ungrateful thought. It doesn't make you a bad or ungrateful person to have a thought like this pop up; instead, it gives you an opportunity to develop your gratitude even further!

Commit to catching yourself in an ungrateful thought. It might take a while for one to pop up, and it might take a few tries before you realize your thought is ungrateful and catch it as it's happening. Don't give up, you'll catch one eventually!

When you do catch an ungrateful thought, write it down or type it out on your computer or smartphone. Really flesh it out and make sure you've captured the essence of the thought.

Now, flip the thought! Think about the core of the thought and consider what you have to be grateful for instead of what you can complain about. Write this flipped thought down.

For example, perhaps your ungrateful thought was about your significant other forgetting to do something really important that you asked them to do. To flip this thought, think about how grateful you are to have a good relationship with your significant other, or to have a healthy romantic relationship at all.

This exercise won't excuse or deny the things that upset you, but it will offer a counterpoint to any ungrateful thought and balance your perspective.

PRACTICE IMMEDIATE GRATITUDE

This exercise will help you practice gratitude in the moment, right here and right now. It can give you a quick boost of gratitude and put you in the right frame of mind to be on the lookout for things to be grateful for as you continue your day.

Wherever you are right now, pause (unless you're driving—in that case, wait until you get to a place where you can park!) and look around you. Notice one thing that you enjoy looking at, which is pretty or interesting, or one thing that you are grateful for.

Focus on this object. Direct all of your attention to enjoying whatever aspect of it is most pleasing. If it's a work of art, focus on the beauty of the technique and the combination of colors. If the object you are grateful for is a photograph of a place that is important to you, focus on how wonderful that place is.

Open yourself up and allow this pleasing object to fill you with gratitude and good feelings.

After a few minutes of enjoying this object, shift your focus to the rest of your environment. You'll probably notice that you can suddenly find a lot more things to be grateful for. This is a wonderful result of the immediate gratitude exercise—it makes all the good things around you more noticeable and more prominent.

Try this exercise anytime you need a quick injection of gratitude and positivity.

SCHEDULE 5 MINUTES OF GRATITUDE

It can be tough to find time to be grateful. It seems like we are all so busy rushing through our fully scheduled days that we don't even realize we have no time to stop and practice gratitude!

If you feel like this applies to you, then scheduling some time for gratitude may be just the cure. You can turn a weakness into a strength by harnessing the very practice that makes being grateful difficult and using it to encourage a practice of gratitude.

Set an alarm or schedule 5 minutes into your calendar every day at the same time (when possible). If you have something you must do during your usual time, reschedule your exercise to another 5-minute block.

When your alarm goes off or your reminder pops up, stop and spend those 5 minutes thinking about all the things in your life you are grateful for. If you're having trouble getting started, go for the obvious things first: your health, your family, your friends, your job, a place to live, the food you have to eat, and so on.

You can write them down in your journal, jot them on a scrap of paper, type them up, or just hold them in your mind. Keeping a record of the things you are grateful for is a great idea, but the point of this exercise is simply to spend a few minutes being grateful.

COUNT YOUR COMPLAINTS

The title of this exercise may sound counterintuitive, but it's the work you do after counting your complaints that really matters.

If you frequently find yourself complaining, even if only in your head, this is a good exercise to try. You'll see that the more you complain, the more you'll have to find to be grateful for! It will both encourage you to find things to be grateful for and discourage you from complaining—a win-win!

On a normal day, carry a small notebook or open up a notepad on your phone. Each time you catch yourself complaining, to someone else or just to yourself, place a mark on your notebook or digital notepad. When you get to five, put a diagonal line through the previous four and move on to a new set of five (this makes it easier to count them up).

At the end of the day, count up your total number of complaints. To counteract this burden of negativity, you're going to balance the complaints with thoughts of gratitude.

However many complaints you had, come up with an equal number of things to be grateful for. If you counted twenty complaints, write twenty things you are grateful for in your journal or notebook.

Regularly practicing this exercise will have the biggest impact on your gratitude, but even doing it once in a while will help you open your eyes to your negativity and encourage you to be more positive.

CHAPTER 6

EXERCISES TO BOOST CONFIDENCE

Ask any therapist about the most common problems that drive patients to their offices, and you're sure to hear that issues with confidence and self-esteem are among them. If you feel like you're lacking in self-confidence, you're not alone! Even the most confident person on earth has at least one or two insecurities.

As common as it is to feel self-conscious or bad about yourself, it's still not a pleasant experience. It can make things like job interviews, work presentations, and dates much more difficult than they need to be. If you are struggling with negative thoughts about yourself or simply experiencing a lack of confidence, give these exercises a try. Some of them are bound to give you that boost in self-confidence that you're looking for!

CHALLENGE YOUR INNER CRITIC

We all have an inner critic, one whose full-time job seems to be finding our greatest insecurities and seeing how often it can bring them up! A little self-judgment from time to time isn't a bad thing—it can get you motivated to do something or serve as a warning that you are not living according to your values. However, when your inner critic begins to pop up too often and flings only insults instead of constructive criticism, it's time to silence it.

The next time you find yourself being overly self-critical, challenge that little voice! Confront it and remind it of all the times it has been wrong. If it's needling you about screwing up on an assignment at work, contradict it by listing all the times you successfully completed such an assignment.

If your inner critic is telling you that you'll surely blow your upcoming date with someone new, remind it how many times a date you were nervous about turned out great. If that feels too inauthentic, try reminding it how many times you've success-fully interacted with people in general.

It's difficult to challenge your inner critic at first but you'll get better with practice. Recognizing when your critic is active may be the most difficult part, so don't give up too early! Stay committed to rooting out the little naysayer, and you'll see a boost in your confidence.

STRIKE A CONFIDENT POSTURE

Have you noticed the connection between posture and confidence? If not, pay attention next time you're feeling more or less confident than usual. You'll probably notice that your shoulders are hunched and your back is slumped when you're feeling less confident; you might cross your legs and/or your arms, taking up as little space as possible. When you feel confident, you might notice that you sit up a little straighter, your shoulders are drawn back, and you stretch out and take up more space. How confident you feel in the moment influences your posture in the moment—so could your posture also influence your confidence?

The next time you're feeling self-conscious, try striking one of these confident postures:

* Stand up straight with legs hip-width apart. Ball your hands into fists and put them on your hips. Tilt your chin up, as if you were looking at something just over the horizon.
* Stand up straight with legs hip-width apart. Raise your arms in a "V" position, or as you would for the "Y" in "YMCA."
* Sit at a desk or table with your legs hip-width apart. Lean forward slightly, rest your elbows on the table, and fold your hands together in front of your chest, knuckles facing up.

Keep this exercise in mind, especially before a big presentation, job interview, or another nerve-racking situation.

SHOW YOUR PEARLY WHITES

Like body language, facial expressions are also tied to how you feel. You flash a genuine smile when you're feeling good, and don a scowl when you're upset. If your feelings can affect your facial expressions so easily, perhaps your facial expressions can influence your feelings!

To give it a shot, all you have to do is smile.

However, not just any smile will do; there are a few guidelines to help you do it right. You may be thinking, "Why would I need guidelines to smile?" Of course, no one needs to be taught to smile, but a forced smile is not the same as an authentic smile.

Here's how you can imitate an authentic smile:

* When you smile, allow the skin at the corners of your eyes to crinkle.
* Don't force your eyes to stay wide open—it's okay if they squint a bit.
* Show your teeth! Let your lips part and smile with your teeth showing.

If you have trouble with following these guidelines, there is a cheat: you can hold a pencil between your teeth! Holding the pencil in your mouth (horizontally) and gripping the pencil with your teeth pushes your mouth into the authentic smile position. When you just can't conjure up an authentic smile, give the pencil a try instead.

With either option, hold your smile for 1 minute and enjoy the confidence boost!

TRY ON A NEW PERSONA

If you've ever been in a school play or dabbled in amateur the-ater, you may have noticed something interesting: even if you're feeling anxious about your performance before you take the stage, that anxiety usually drops as you slide into your role. There's something about playing a role that makes it easier to put yourself out there; you have another persona to tap into, so you don't have room for all the anxiety anymore. Luckily, you don't have to try out for the local community theater group to reap the benefits of this phenomenon.

For this exercise, come up with an alternate, confident per-sona. If you have a favorite heroic character from a movie or book, you can use him or her as your alternate persona. Go with whatever works for you; just make sure the persona you decide on is confident and self-assured.

Once you've chosen your alternate persona, go out and give it a test run. Engage in a situation or activity that you usu-ally dread or that you feel nervous about, but go into it with your alternate persona.

If you find your persona doesn't make you feel confident or is inappropriate for the situation, come up with a new one and try that persona instead. It may take a few tries, but you will find a persona that gives you an immediate confidence boost. Use this persona to "fake it 'til you make it," and eventually you won't even need the persona anymore.

DO SOMETHING EMBARRASSING

Paradoxically, doing something intentionally embarrassing can actually enhance your sense of self-confidence. If you do something embarrassing but find that you survive, or even end up laughing at yourself, the fear of looking foolish won't have as much power over you. It might feel uncomfortable, scary, or downright terrifying, but you *will* come out the other side unscathed!

There are many ways to practice this exercise, but here are two popular ones that can help you get started:

1. Go to a crowded area, like the mall during the holiday season or the bank when it has a long line. Without any prompting or lead-up, simply look at your watch and loudly announce the time. After this, go about your business as if nothing out of the ordinary just happened.

2. Go to a store—any store—and ask the cashier where to find something that you know the store doesn't carry. For example, go to an auto parts store and ask the employee behind the counter to bring you a copy of today's newspaper, or go to an electronics store and ask the cashier where you can find the cat food.

This exercise is extremely easy to do in terms of the actual steps you need to take, but at the same time, it can be very difficult to get over the mental block! As anxiety-inducing as it can be, steel your nerves and give it a try. You'll survive, and you'll enjoy a rush of post-embarrassment adrenaline to boot!

GET UNCOMFORTABLE

These days, it seems there are endless technologies, applications, and gadgets intended to make us more comfortable. Everywhere you look, offices are buying ergonomic furniture and car companies are offering an ever-increasing number of ways to customize your car seat to your exact liking. This isn't a bad thing—it's good to minimize your aches and pains! However, the focus on comfort can backfire in other areas.

Self-confidence is one area in which too much comfort is actually a bad thing. Although it's easy and safe to stay in your comfort zone, you don't learn or grow without a challenge. When you never challenge yourself, you never get a chance to see what you are really capable of, and this leads you to doubt your abilities and even question your worth.

To make sure you don't fall into this self-esteem trap, give the uncomfortable exercise a try!

The next time an opportunity comes up that (a) you believe would be beneficial for you, and (b) you know would make you uncomfortable, seize the opportunity!

If you get invited to a networking event with people from your field who would be good to know, accept the invitation. If your high school reunion is coming up and you'd love to see your old friends (and maybe an old flame), but you're afraid it will be awkward, go anyway!

You don't need to stay all night, but you may find that, once you get there and begin to loosen up, you will want to stay after all.

MAKE A CONFIDENCE LIST

Sometimes all your self-confidence needs is a little reminder to get it up and running again. Spending just a few minutes crafting such a reminder can do wonders for your sense of confidence in yourself.

Get out your trusty notebook or journal and prepare to make a new entry. Next, write the following headers:

* At the top of the next blank page, write "Ten Things I Am Good At."
* At the top of the page after, write "Ten Reasons I Am Proud of Myself."
* At the top of the third page, write "Ten Things That Make Me a Good Person."

List the ten items under each column. It might feel uncomfortable at first, but it's important to have a realistic idea of your strengths and positive qualities if you want to increase your confidence.

If you have trouble coming up with any of the items for this list, pause and ask yourself what your partner, your mother, or your best friend would put in each column. In fact, if you're feeling really stuck, call him or her up and ask! Often those closest to you know things about you that you can't see or don't even think about.

Put some serious thought into these lists and you will have a great resource to flip back to whenever you need a quick boost of confidence.

THINK ABOUT YOUR JOURNEY

The hero's journey is a popular theme in literature—perhaps the *most* popular theme in literature. There's something about the story of a brave protagonist facing trials and tribulations, and ultimately overcoming them, that resonates with people. We find it easy to identify with the hero, because we, too, have faced challenges and come out the other side stronger and wiser.

The hero often starts out as an underdog, which makes it easy for us to root for her. She must learn lessons and gain skills to overcome her obstacles. If she faced the story's final challenge when we met her at the beginning of the story, she would fail miserably.

In our lives, we are the hero; each of us is the protagonist of our own story. We are all on our own journey, in which we must gain skills and learn lessons in order to grow. When you are feeling self-conscious or down about yourself, keep this in mind. Cast yourself as the protagonist in a story about a hero's journey.

We accept that it takes the hero time and effort to learn the skills, knowledge, and abilities that allow her to succeed; however, for some reason, we often find it hard to accept this simple fact in ourselves. Remind yourself that the hero gradually gains all the tools and knowledge she needs, rather than starting out with everything at hand.

Sometimes all you need to boost your confidence is to shift your perspective!

KILL ONE BAD HABIT

We all feel down about ourselves on occasion, but if your lack of self-confidence is dragging you down, kick-start it by doing something good for yourself.

In this case, the good thing you can do for yourself is to ditch one bad habit—just one, and it should be a small one. For example, maybe your bad habit is that you bite your fingernails. Or you might indulge in a high-calorie three p.m. snack every day or fall asleep without brushing your teeth every night.

Whatever your small bad habit is, defeating it will give you a boost of confidence in yourself. If you can conquer your own worst behaviors, you can conquer anything!

If you're having trouble ditching a bad habit, come up with a plan of action. This plan should break your goal into smaller, more manageable steps and reward you for your progress. For instance, if your bad habit is snacking on something unhealthy every afternoon, you could make a plan to taper off (e.g., eat it four days this week, then three days next week, then two days the week after that, and so on) and reward yourself with something healthy that you enjoy.

If all else fails and you are still struggling to kick your bad habit, try tackling a smaller habit first.

SET A SMALL GOAL

If your confidence is flagging and you notice that you don't believe in yourself as much as you used to, it's a good time to give this exercise a try. Setting, striving toward, and achieving a small goal is a great way to remind yourself what you are capable of and restore your faith in your own abilities.

Keep the SMART acronym in mind when setting your goal; in other words, your goal should be:

* **S**pecific: don't set a vague goal like "Get healthy." Set something more specific, like "Lose 15 pounds."
* **M**easurable: your goal should be measurable, so you can tell when you've achieved it; for example, "Lose 15 pounds" is measurable, while "Lose weight" is not.
* **A**ttainable: setting a goal you can never reach is setting yourself up for disappointment; at the same time, setting a goal that takes no effort to meet is pointless! Aim for somewhere in the middle.
* **R**elevant: although small, your goal should still be relevant to you and your life; it should feed into your larger goals and the general direction you would like to take your life.
* **T**ime-bound (or time-limited): your goal needs to have a timer; if you set a goal with no deadline, you won't feel any sense of urgency to work toward it.

Use these guidelines to set a small, realistic, and relevant goal for yourself, work toward it, and bask in the satisfaction of your success!

CROSS IT OFF YOUR TO-DO LIST

You know that to-do list you have, the one you have written on paper, typed on your laptop, or simply floating around your head? The one you've had for weeks, months, or even longer? The one with those things that you'll "get around to" eventually? It's time to address one of those items!

Crossing just one thing off your to-do list can have an astonishing impact on how you feel about yourself.

Right now, pull out your to-do list. If it's on your computer, take a moment to pull it up. If it's in your notebook or journal, go grab it. If it's in your head, write it down. If you don't even *have* a to-do list, make one! There has to be at least one or two things you've been meaning to get to, right?

Now, take a look at your list. Choose one thing on your list that you can do today—right here, right now. If there are multiple things you could do immediately, choose the one that you want to cross off your list the most.

This one simple action will show you that you can get things done when you put your mind to it and remind you how good it feels to get them done! Don't be surprised if you find that you suddenly have the time and energy for the other items on your to-do list as well.

MAKE A CONFIDENCE COLLAGE

This exercise is a bit more involved than many of the others, but it's also a fun activity with a long-term impact. You'll especially enjoy this exercise if you like doing creative arts and crafts.

Sometimes when you find yourself feeling unconfident and doubtful of your abilities, it's because you've lost sight of what's important. You might be forgetting to live by your true values, procrastinating on your goals, or neglecting your best skills and abilities.

This exercise will help you remind yourself of what is most important to you and encourage you to work toward a future in which you are happy and confident.

All you'll need is a piece of poster board, some glue or tape, a few photographs, and some magazines (or a search engine and a printer if you have no magazines lying around).

Take some time to think about what you value most and what your biggest goals are, and then peruse your photographs, flip through the magazines, and search online for images that represent or support them.

Cut out or print these images or copy the photos, and put your creative mind to work arranging them on your poster board. Feel free to use markers, paint, stickers, sticky notes, glitter, ribbons, or anything else that helps you make your collage look appealing and feel authentic.

Once it's done, hang it in your bedroom or another room you visit several times a day. Every time you look at it, draw inspiration from your cherished values and important goals.

CREATE CONFIDENCE AFFIRMATIONS

Affirmations are a great way to give yourself a boost of confidence in any given moment. Sometimes all you need to feel good about yourself and get on with your day is a gentle reminder of the goodness that exists within you.

To get started, write a list of positive and uplifting statements about yourself.

Follow these guidelines:

1. Write them in the present tense. Craft statements that affirm your value right now—not your potential value tomorrow, next week, or next year.
2. Use a first-person perspective. Don't write statements about yourself as if you were someone else; write them from your own point of view.
3. Focus on your positive qualities and the traits you want to enhance.

Some examples of confidence affirmations include:

* "I am happy with who I am."
* "I do great and valuable work."
* "I am confident in my own skin."

Be sure to repeat your affirmations once a day, but don't limit yourself to once a day! You can practice your affirmations as often as needed to boost your self-esteem.

QUIT MAKING UNEVEN COMPARISONS

You've probably heard that it's unhealthy and unhelpful to compare yourself with others too much. It's true—constant comparison is bound to leave you feeling frustrated and self-conscious. However, it's not necessarily the act of comparing that is so harmful. It might be that you're making uneven comparisons.

This is a simple but profound truth that has the potential to trigger an "aha!" moment: when you compare yourself with others, you are often comparing their strengths to your weaknesses. You rarely compare your strengths to their weaknesses, or your strengths to their strengths; instead, you jump straight to the comparison with the higher disparity and the unfavorable skew.

It is these uneven comparisons that are damaging to your self-confidence and self-esteem, and pretty useless to boot. After all, what do you gain by comparing yourself with others on things you struggle with, but they excel at? What valuable insight does this give you, beyond reminding you that you have weaknesses and others have strengths? You already know that!

A comparison that could actually produce useful insight would consider your strengths and the strengths of others, or your weaknesses and the weaknesses of others.

Keep this tendency to make uneven comparisons in mind the next time you think about how you measure up to others, and make sure that any comparisons you do make are on more of an even playing field.

CHAPTER 7

EXERCISES TO DEVELOP MINDFULNESS

Mindfulness is a hot topic in both research and self-help materials right now. Everywhere you look, you can find a mindfulness program, a book on mindfulness, a mindfulness speaker series, or classes on increasing mindfulness. It may have all the hallmarks of a fad that will soon fade away, but the benefits are for real. Mindfulness has been linked to tons of positive outcomes, including improved health, happiness, and well-being.

Luckily, it's also really easy to do! You don't need any special equipment or technology to do it (although some people find an app helpful). All you need is yourself, a little bit of time, and a place to sit. These exercises will walk you through some of the many ways to practice mindfulness.

TRY BASIC MINDFULNESS

To ease yourself into a mindfulness practice, try this:

1. Take 10 or 15 minutes for yourself and find a quiet spot to sit. It's best to find at least a somewhat comfortable seat. Close your eyes if that feels right.
2. Begin to notice your thoughts. You're not attempting to stop them, avoid them, or change them—only to notice them as they go by. Stay in the present moment instead of letting your mind linger on the past or future.
3. When any judgments (e.g., "should" statements, self-criticism) arise, avoid the urge to either latch on to them or push them away; simply notice them, make note of them, and let them pass.
4. If you find your mind wandering from the present moment, gently guide it back. Avoid scolding yourself; just bring yourself back to the present.
5. Once you feel totally in tune with the present moment, take at least 1 or 2 minutes to simply "be." Feel free to stay here longer if you'd like.
6. When you feel ready, bring yourself gently back. Open your eyes and go on with your day, but try to carry that sense of present-moment awareness with you.

This can be a wonderful experience on its own, but it will bring you the most benefits when you engage in a regular, consistent practice of mindfulness.

OBSERVE AN OBJECT

In this exercise, you will observe an object. Sounds easy, right? Well, yes and no!

It's easy in that all you have to do is look at and feel an object, but it might not be so easy to keep your attention on it for the entire 5 minutes.

Pick an object that is near you right now. It doesn't matter what it is, but it's best if the object is interesting for some reason—an unusual shape, a pleasant design, or a fun texture (you get bonus mindfulness points if it's something natural, like a leaf or an acorn).

Once you have chosen your object, pick it up (or just touch it if it's too big to pick up). Note the current time, or set an alarm with a gentle ringer, and give the object your full attention for 5 minutes.

Notice the color of the object. Notice if there's a design or a pattern, or if it's solid throughout. Notice if it's made up of many colors.

Notice the shape of the object—whether it's round or square, whether it has hard corners or soft edges.

Notice the texture of the object. Pay attention to the way it feels to touch it, and whether it is one texture throughout or many.

Continue focusing on the object until your alarm sounds. You'll find that you are more in tune with the present moment and more aware of what is happening both within you and outside of you.

PRACTICE MINDFUL EATING

Food lovers rejoice! This exercise is all about fully experiencing and savoring your food.

First, grab something to eat. Pick something you can eat with your hands, like an apple or a peach.

Hold it in your hands. Study the surface, noticing the shape and color. Look to see if it has a pattern or a grain to it.

Feel the food with your fingers. Notice the texture, whether it's hard or soft, rough or smooth. Notice the weight of it in your hands.

Next, move to smelling it. Hold it to your nose and inhale deeply. Take a few breaths like this and experience the scent.

Now, take a bite. Pay attention to how hard you need to bite in order to get a reasonably sized piece. Notice the texture against your lips and the inside of your cheeks and the roof of your mouth. Feel the texture with your tongue.

Notice the taste, whether it's sweet or sharp or tangy or salty. Be aware of whether the taste changes as you eat—perhaps it's tart at first, but the taste mellows out as you chew.

Continue eating mindfully until you have finished your food. Repeat this exercise as often as you'd like to boost your mindfulness practice.

SORT YOUR THOUGHTS

Sometimes we can get overwhelmed by our thoughts. We have so many thoughts and feelings and sensations running through our head, it's a wonder we get anything done! If you've been feeling overwhelmed by your thoughts, give organizing your thoughts a try.

You won't need any paper or a writing implement for this, as all the organizing will happen in your mind.

Find a quiet spot and sit in a comfortable seat. Close your eyes, and allow yourself to sink into the present moment. Observe your thoughts as they come and go.

Once you feel fully engaged in the present moment, envision three buckets. Label one "Thoughts," one "Feelings," and the third "Sensations."

As your thoughts arise, consider them and decide which bucket they fit in.

For example, if the thought "I'm still sore from yoga the other day" arises, you would move it to the "Sensations" bucket. If the thought "I'm excited to see the movie tonight" pops up, you would move it to the "Feelings" bucket. If the thought "I wonder how long I've been doing this" comes up, you would move it to the "Thoughts" bucket.

Continue sorting your thoughts for 5 to 10 minutes.

This exercise will force you to focus on the present, since it's very difficult to think about the past or future while sorting your current thoughts!

MIND YOUR BREATH

Mindful breathing is a great way to dip your toes into mindfulness. It's quick, it's easy, and all you need to do is breathe!

Find a comfortable seat or lie down in a comfortable position. Close your eyes or keep your gaze soft and relaxed.

Start with a few deep breaths. Breathe in deeply through your nose, counting to five as you go. Pause and hold the air in your lungs for a moment or two, then breathe out through your nose, counting to five as you exhale. When your lungs are empty, pause again for a moment or two, then begin the next breath.

Next, return to your normal breath. Breathe in and out as you normally do, and pay attention to your body as you breathe. Notice how your chest and your belly feel as you breathe in and out.

Be aware of your body. Take note of any sensations in your legs. Feel the weight of your body in the chair or on the floor. If there are any areas where you are holding tension, relax them.

Turn your attention back to your breath. Focus on the breaths you take, following the end of each breath into the beginning of the next. If your mind begins to wander, turn it gently back to your breath.

After a few minutes, gradually bring yourself back to the present moment. Thank yourself for taking the time for mindful breathing and continue on with your day.

TRY A QUICK MINDFULNESS MEDITATION

If you're ready to dive in to mindfulness and you have at least 10 minutes or so to spare, give mindfulness meditation a try.

Follow these steps to engage in mindfulness meditation:

1. Set aside 10 or 15 minutes, and find a quiet spot to sit. It's best to find a somewhat comfortable seat. Close your eyes if that feels right.
2. Open up your awareness to your body. Notice the position of your legs and any sensations in your lower body.
3. Notice the position and sensations of your upper body. Straighten your back to a comfortable but upright posture. Place your palms on your knees or anywhere on your thighs that feels comfortable.
4. Pay attention to your breath. Notice the rhythm of your breath as you draw the air into your lungs and gently exhale it. Notice the way your chest rises and falls with each breath. If your focus slips, gently bring it back to your breath.
5. Don't direct your thoughts to anything in particular, and don't worry if your mind wanders. Simply observe the thoughts that come up, and let them pass by.
6. When you're ready to move on with your day, gently open your eyes and shift your awareness to your body and your immediate environment.

Repeat as often as you can to keep up a regular practice.

HEIGHTEN YOUR AWARENESS

This is a great exercise to boost your awareness and get you to practice mindfulness every day. You will take a simple, every-day task and turn it into a reminder to be mindful and grateful in every moment.

You can start with one task and build up the habit, then add tasks to your list as you desire.

Think of something you do many times a day. It could be buckling your seat belt, washing your hands, or checking your phone for messages. Whichever activity you choose, try to remember that it is a signal for mindfulness as you go about your day.

Whenever you engage in this activity, take a moment to be mindful and grateful for the abilities that allow you to engage in it. For example, if you chose buckling your seat belt, remember to pause as you buckle yourself in. Think of all the things that allow you to buckle your seat belt and, ultimately, to drive: legs that work the gas and brake pedals, arms to steer, good eye-sight that allows you to see the road ahead of you, and so on. Be grateful for all of these abilities.

Engaging in this exercise will help you weave mindfulness into your everyday life, and it can give you a little gratitude boost as the cherry on top!

LISTEN MINDFULLY

You know that feeling you get when you're talking to some-one and you can see their eyes glazing over? You know they're physically present, but their mind might be wandering very, very far. It's not a good feeling! We all occasionally allow our minds to wander instead of listening attentively, but if you find yourself drifting off frequently, this exercise can help you train your brain to stay on task!

To give mindful listening a try, all you need is some head-phones and a piece of music you have never listened to before.

1. Put your headphones on, turn the volume up to a comfortable level, and close your eyes (if that feels comfortable).
2. Do your best to forget who the artist is, when the music was recorded, what genre it fits into, or any other bit of information you know about the music. Make an effort to empty your mind of any knowledge that could bias you in one way or another.
3. Once you feel your head is clear (or as clear as it can be), focus on the music. Notice the mix of instruments, the rise and fall of the notes, the pitch and the tone. Pour yourself into the music and focus all of your attention on the experience.

Practice listening mindfully to one track each day, and you will find it easier and easier to focus your attention on listening to anything you choose to attend to.

MAKE MINDFUL TRANSITIONS

With the ultra-packed schedules and multiple commitments of life today, it can be tempting to rush straight from one task or activity to the next. When you have a million things to get done, it's hard to justify taking even the smallest break; however, this approach leads to distraction and stress, making you ultimately less effective.

By spending just a few moments shifting your mind-set from one task to the next, you can improve your mindfulness and improve your efficiency.

Commit to trying this technique for one whole day. Each time you find yourself about to switch from one task to the next (e.g., from parking at work to preparing to start your workday, moving from finishing up a report to working on a spreadsheet), follow these steps:

1. Pause, even if you're in a hurry. It will only take a few moments!
2. Mentally confirm that you are done with the task you were just doing. Put it completely aside.
3. Focus on your breathing for five breaths. If your breathing is rapid or irregular, try counting to five on the inhale, pausing for 2 seconds, counting to five on the exhale, and pausing for 2 seconds again.
4. Mentally shift gears to the task you are about to start.

This extremely simple exercise can have a big impact on how calm and focused you feel, and it only takes a few minutes!

TAKE A MINDFUL DRIVE

You can practice driving mindfully anytime, but you will likely find it easier to do with an empty car and a little bit of time to spare before you need to get where you're going.

Whether you're on your way to work, the grocery store, or nowhere in particular, give the following exercise a try:

1. After you get in the driver's seat and shut the door, turn off your phone and silence the radio. Take a few moments to simply sit and be. You can focus on your breathing if you need something to direct your attention to.
2. Look around you and open your eyes to the details of your environment. What do you see, beyond the concrete and asphalt? Leafy trees? Grass waving in the breeze? Couples walking hand in hand? Allow yourself to notice these things.
3. Continue examining your surroundings and noticing any thoughts or sensations that arise as you drive (carefully, of course). Whenever you get to a stoplight, take the opportunity to engage in a few mindful breaths.
4. When you reach your destination, turn the car off and take another few moments to simply sit and be. Express your gratitude that you arrived safely, and take a few final deep, mindful breaths.

Try to practice mindful driving at least once every few days.

TAKE A FRESH LOOK

Sometimes all it takes to make you more mindful is experiencing something new. A new object, especially something particularly interesting or unusual, can draw all of your attention and ground you firmly in the present.

You could use this fact as an excuse to do frequent shopping—it seems like there's always something new out there that you could use! However, a more challenging (and cost-effective) way to take advantage of this phenomenon is to practice looking at old, familiar objects through a new perspective.

Find a familiar object in your immediate environment, like your cell phone, a child's toy, or a three-hole punch.

Now, take a fresh look at the object; in other words, pretend you have never seen this object before. If you had never seen this object before, what would you think it was? What details would you notice?

Pay attention to the shape, color, pattern or design, texture, weight, and any other salient details. Think about what the function of the piece might be, or how you could see yourself using it. If it helps, look at it through a young child's eyes; pretending you have no knowledge of how the object works may help you to see all of the details you usually miss.

Cultivating a practice of taking a fresh look at things around you will help you to become more aware and observant, but it may also enhance your sense of gratitude for the things you have.

IMMERSE YOURSELF

A quintessential mindfulness exercise involves immersing yourself completely in an activity. We so often engage in our tasks and activities with divided attention and our minds on other things.

Think about it—how often do you actually focus on what you are doing when you wash the dishes, pack a lunch, or pay your bills? Even when you are doing things you enjoy, you still allow your mind to wander and your focus to slip away.

You can practice keeping your attention on the present moment by immersing yourself in your current activity. For this exercise, it doesn't matter if you enjoy the activity or not; we all have to do things we don't particularly enjoy, and there's no reason why we can't make these a more joyful or more pleasant experience, or at least a more effective use of our time.

Whatever you are doing, commit to experiencing every moment of it. Dedicate yourself to it 100 percent, and challenge yourself to do it well.

Pay attention to every detail of your activity. For example, if you are balancing your checkbook, open up your awareness to the soft scratch of your pen on paper, the feel of the case on your checkbook beneath your fingers, and the mental math you are doing to make the numbers match up.

Try this exercise, and you may just find yourself amazed at how much more efficient and joyful you are in completing your task!

SET AN INTENTION

If you've ever cultivated a regular yoga practice or participated in an instructor-led yoga class, you're probably familiar with the idea of setting an intention for your practice. Your intention can be anything you'd like it to be, from paying special attention to a particular part of your body to nurturing a sense of gratitude for everything you have. Recalling your intention can help you reorient yourself in the session if your mind begins to wander or help you to focus on your goals.

Similar to setting an intention in yoga, setting an intention for your day can help you stay focused on achieving your goals and keep your perspective at the right level.

Set your intention as soon as you get up, before you begin your undoubtedly busy day. Your intention can be anything you like—finishing up a project at work, remembering to pick up the dry cleaning, or sitting down to watch that movie you promised your kids you would watch with them.

The only stipulation on your intention is that it must be something you absolutely intend to accomplish today; save your toughest challenges and long-term goals for another time, and focus on completing something realistic for your intention today.

If, during the course of your day, you find yourself unmotivated or off task, remind yourself of your commitment to your intention, and let it give you the boost you need to get things done!

DO A BODY SCAN

This exercise is an extremely popular one in mindfulness circles. It offers you a chance to practice mindfulness and mindful breathing, ease tense or sore muscles, and generally shed some of your stress. Best of all, the main thing you need to give it a try is a quiet place to lie down and stretch out! Your bed works well for this exercise, of course, but the floor can also work just as well with a blanket or yoga mat to cushion you.

To do the body scan, follow these steps:

1. Lie on your back and close your eyes.
2. Starting with your toes, focus your attention on one area of your body at a time. Notice the sensations in that area, noting whether there is any tension or soreness.
3. Direct your breath at any tension or soreness you find. Visualize the discomfort leaving your body, whether it leaves by evaporating, melting, getting scooped away, or simply floating up out of your body. Feel the relaxation settle in its place.
4. Move your awareness through every area of your body, from your feet up to the top of your head.

Practice this exercise whenever you are feeling particularly tense or stressed, and you are sure to feel a bit calmer and more centered at the end.

CHAPTER 8

EXERCISES TO ENHANCE YOUR STRENGTHS

Strength-based development is increasingly popular, both for personal development and for professional development. Organizations are paying more attention to their employees' strengths than ever, and spending valuable resources on helping them to continue building and enhancing their strengths. While this is great for employees, organizations aren't doing it out of the goodness of their hearts; they've found that it actually boosts their bottom line as well.

If you'd like to get in on this exciting new trend, this is the perfect chapter for you. You will find exercises on identifying your unique strengths, exercises to help you plan out uses for—and the development of—your strengths, and exercises to take your top strengths to the next level.

GATHER FEEDBACK ON YOUR STRENGTHS

This probably won't surprise you, but the first step in enhancing your strengths is to find out what they are! There are several ways to identify your strengths, including taking questionnaires and filling out surveys, getting feedback from a variety of sources, and doing some serious self-reflection. The method described here involves asking some of the people closest to you about what strengths they have observed in you.

Come up with a list of at least five or six people from all areas of your life: your manager, coworkers at your current job, coworkers and managers from your old jobs, your parents, your professors or mentors, your friends, and anyone else you think has seen you at your best or in roles in which you thrived.

Compose an email or letter to these people explaining that you are hoping to learn about your own strengths. Ask them what they believe your strengths are, and request examples of times when they saw your strengths in action. Be sure to thank them for their time, even before they begin.

Once you receive their feedback, comb through it to identify any common traits or skills mentioned by multiple sources. The most commonly mentioned strengths are likely your greatest strengths, along with any others that at least two or three people pointed out.

This exercise is a good one if you have trouble with self-reflection or have a negative self-image, since you build your strengths profile based on feedback from others.

JOURNAL TO FIND YOUR STRENGTHS

This exercise uses journaling to help you figure out where your greatest strengths lie.

Get a journal or a notebook and commit to writing in it each day for at least one week.

1. Each night, write down every activity you engaged in throughout your day. Include every activity that is not a basic necessity sort of task (e.g., eating, brushing your teeth). Write down things you do at work, like running a meeting or evaluating performance. Write things you do around the house, like tidying up or fixing the sink. Perhaps most importantly, write things you do in your free time, like painting or cycling.

2. At the end of the week, gather all of your activities onto one sheet and note how many times you engaged in each.

3. Next, think about how much you enjoyed doing each of these activities, and rate your enjoyment on a scale from 1 (hate it) to 7 (would do it all day if you could).

4. Finally, rate your effectiveness in each activity on a scale from 1 (terrible at it) to 7 (you could make a living teaching others how to do it).

5. Add the two numbers together to make a score between 2 and 14.

Whenever you engage in an activity that is a 12 or higher, you're using one of your strengths.

MONITOR YOUR MOOD

One of the best ways to identify your unique strengths requires nothing more than paying attention to your mood!

Observe yourself for a day or two, paying close attention to how you feel when you do various activities.

So, how do you know if you're using your strengths? Look for these signs:

* You are excited and full of energy.
* You feel engaged and motivated.
* You lose track of time because you're so focused on what you're doing.
* You are more outgoing or confident than usual.

When you use your strengths, you tend to feel good! You get excited and energetic when you're enthusiastic about what you're doing, and you feel engaged and motivated when you care about what you're doing.

If you regularly get so absorbed that you lose track of time during an activity, you are likely using one of your top strengths. Likewise, if you get a boost of confidence when you engage in a task, you are probably putting one of your strengths to use.

Look for instances where you notice all four of these signs; these instances are when you are using your top strengths. Instances where you notice two or three signs are likely indicators that you are using another of your strengths.

Figure out what it is that makes you feel this way, and the relevant strength will practically identify itself!

SELF-REFLECT ON YOUR STRENGTHS

Self-reflection is good for so many things, including getting to know yourself better, finding out what is most important to you, and identifying problem areas in your life. Now, you can add identifying, planning for, and developing your strengths to that list, because in this exercise you will use self-reflection to do just that!

Grab a journal or notebook if you don't have one already, or a simple piece of paper will do. Write down these five questions, and take a few minutes to reflect on each one before answering:

1. What are your top strengths? If you need help identifying your strengths, see one of the previous exercises in this chapter.
2. How can your top strengths be applied to better your life and the lives of others?
3. How can holding back your top strengths inhibit you or make life more difficult for you and those around you?
4. What do you need to do to fully embrace your strengths?
5. How can those around you best support you in developing and applying your strengths?

Use your answers to these questions to figure out what your top strengths are and how you currently use them, and to come up with a plan to develop them even further.

IMAGINE YOUR BEST POSSIBLE SELF

This exercise can help you set goals for your future, determine which strengths you will need to cultivate to get there, and motivate you to put in the time and effort to improve yourself. As an added bonus, it can also boost your sense of hope and optimism!

Grab your journal or a notebook and set aside a few minutes to sit in a quiet place and think. Settle on a specific point in the future (such as six months from now, five years from now, or even ten years from now) and imagine yourself at this point in time; however, instead of thinking about how your life will most likely be at this point, imagine your *best possible* life and *best possible* self at this point.

Imagine that you are meeting or have met all of your goals, you are successful and happy, and you have your dream job, a wonderful relationship with your loved ones, fulfilling hobbies, and/or anything else that is important to you. Note as much detail as possible, and paint as vivid a picture as you can of your future self.

Now, think about the strengths you will need to apply to get to this point. Will you need to maximize your persistence? Engage in lots of strategic planning? Use some truly excellent people skills?

Write down the strengths, skills, and traits you will need to use to get where you want to be, and commit to enhancing or improving them.

CHART YOUR STRENGTHS

Once you have identified your strengths, you may need help coming up with a plan to improve them. After all, there are a lot of strengths! Which one should you focus on? Should you focus on more than one at a time? Is it best to target your most salient strength, or should you work on one of your lesser strengths?

Completing this exercise will help you determine which strengths you already use regularly and which strengths you underutilize, and decide which strengths offer you the most room for improvement.

Think of your top five or six strengths, and draw the frame for a chart on a sheet of paper. Label the horizontal line with your strengths and the vertical line with the numbers 0 through 10.

For each strength, you will draw two bars: one representing how much you believe you *could* use that strength in your life, and one representing how much you use it currently.

For example, if you think you have a great opportunity to apply your strength for critical thinking in your work, you might draw the potential bar up to 9 or 10. If you feel you use critical thinking quite often already, but not as much as you could use it, you might draw the usage bar up to 7 or 8.

The strengths with the biggest gap between the usage and potential bars are the areas in which you have the greatest room for enhancement and improvement.

FOCUS ON OUTCOMES

One strength that most of us could use a bit of a boost in is cultivating an outcome-focused frame of mind. We so often tend to focus on the problems, issues, and obstacles related to accomplishing what we want to accomplish, rather than focusing on how we can actually get to that point. With this exercise, you can practice your outcome-focused thinking and develop related strengths such as planning, organization, and optimistic thinking.

The next time you find yourself rushing through your day, moving from one task to the next without any breathing space or time to reset in between, follow these steps:

1. Press pause and relax for a few moments! Taking a few deep breaths might help.
2. Define the problem, whether in your head, on paper, or out loud. Make sure you know what you are facing in your next task or challenge.
3. Define the outcome you would like to achieve. Make sure you know where you want to be at the end of your next activity.
4. Connect the dots between where you are and where you'd like to be. If it helps, write out the steps you need to take.

It's that simple! Of course, it's easier to write these steps out than to put them into practice, but you may be surprised at how easy it is to come up with solutions when you organize your thoughts into a more helpful order.

PLAN TOMORROW'S STRENGTHS

If you've ever worked with someone who has a million things to do all the time (or if you're one of those people), you probably found that things that don't make it onto the schedule tend to get ignored! When you have a laundry list of things to do, one or two of them are bound to be forgotten or pushed aside, and those that are not written in pen or marked on your calendar are likely to be the first to be dropped.

Similarly, it's great to decide to develop your strengths, but simply affirming your desire to cultivate a strength is not sufficient to make it happen. To increase the likelihood that you will actually get to working on your strength, it helps to plan it out.

Once you have identified your strengths and determined which one(s) you want to use more often or to greater effect, take a few moments each night to plan your strengths usage the next day.

Identify which strength you will focus on and how you plan to apply it. In addition, spend a minute or two visualizing how you can put it to *best* use.

When you've got a good idea of your plans for the next day, write them down in your notebook or journal. The simple act of writing down what you intend to do makes it much more likely that you will make it a priority once you're in the middle of your busy day.

ADD YOUR STRENGTHS TO A TEAM

One of the best ways to put your strengths to use and develop them further is to apply them to a team or group setting. Not only will you get a chance to enhance your strengths, but you will get the satisfaction of contributing to a successful team and producing high-quality results.

This is easiest to do at work, but if you are not currently working or if you don't work in an environment that is conducive to teams, give it a try with your hobbies, a passion project, or volunteer work.

When you find yourself assigned to a new team or with a new project that requires a team effort, suggest that the entire team makes a commitment to playing to their strengths. This doesn't mean you only get to do the things you like, but that you will discuss each team member's unique strengths and distribute tasks according to them.

Your teammates might be hesitant at first, but you will quickly find that each member has unique likes and dislikes, strengths and weaknesses, and that every team member will be happy to shoulder the responsibility for a task they enjoy in exchange for shedding one they dread taking on.

It might be more work up front to run a team project this way (due to the time needed to identify and discuss each team member's strengths), but it's sure to save time and hassle down the road.

WORK ON YOUR STRENGTHS, NOT YOUR WEAKNESSES

This may be a tough exercise because the assumption that you need to work on your areas of weakness to improve yourself is ingrained in our culture.

You may find much better results by channeling energy into your strengths instead of putting more energy into your weaknesses. This doesn't mean you should avoid meeting the bare minimum for important tasks just because you don't enjoy them; for example, even if you hate writing, you should still be able to write a short, effective communication.

To stop working on your weaknesses, make two lists of activities:

1. Activities you enjoy, that fill you with energy, and that you excel in.
2. Activities you despise or dread, that sap your energy, and that you struggle to perform well.

Commit to doing the activities in the first list much more often and doing the activities in the second list much less often. You can never totally eliminate tasks or activities you don't enjoy from your life, but you can usually find creative ways to do them less often.

For example, if writing is a weakness but working with data is a strength, try to turn activities that require writing into something more like working with data (e.g., making bullet points of salient bits of information instead of writing paragraphs).

COMMIT TO ONE OR TWO STRENGTHS

After determining your top five or six strengths, you may be tempted to dedicate yourself to maximizing all of them. This is probably a mistake! It sounds like working toward improvement in all of your strong areas is a great idea, and it may be over the long term; however, in the short term, all it does is ensure that none of your strengths are getting your full focus.

Once you have identified your strengths, pick one or two near the top and commit to developing these strengths and *only* these strengths, at least for now.

Think about which strength will help you the most in working toward your current goals. Is there one thing in particular that will make achieving your goals easier or faster? This is probably the strength you should commit to right now.

Over the next few months (or even the next year or two), keep this strength (or couple of strengths) in mind, and look for any opportunity to further develop it. If you're thinking of taking on a new project at work, ask yourself what project will help you develop this strength. If you're considering a course or training, sign up for it only if it is related to the one or two strengths you are focusing on right now.

You'll have time for building your other strengths later, but you will likely find it much easier to develop your strengths if you focus on one or two at a time.

MAKE USEFUL COMPARISONS

Most of us find it all too easy to compare ourselves with others. It's a natural urge to want to know how you stack up against those around you, but in terms of strengths development, it's not particularly helpful. There is a much better method of comparison, which involves comparing yourself to the best point of reference: you at another point in time!

Instead of comparing yourself to others with similar strengths, use your own performance in the past to determine whether you are making progress on your strengths. Keep these three rules for comparisons in mind:

* Only compare yourself with yourself; everyone has different strengths at different levels, and it usually doesn't help to compare yourself with others.
* Make comparisons on several bases, including weekly, monthly, and annually; you may not see much improvement in your strengths week by week, but you should see some encouraging results on a more long-term comparison!
* Never compare yourself against a vague image of a future "perfect" version of yourself; you will never be perfect, so avoid the urge to compare yourself against an ideal that will never come to fruition.

Following these guidelines for comparisons will help you to stay on track in your strengths development, make healthy progress, and avoid getting discouraged by unhelpful comparisons.

IDENTIFY THE STRENGTHS OF OTHERS

It's necessary to identify your own strengths in order to improve them, but it can also be extremely useful to identify the strengths of those around you.

Have you ever been on a team with someone who seems to have the exact opposite approach? That experience can be a difficult one. It can be very hard to reach consensus and meet goals when two or more team members have diametrically opposed approaches for getting the work done! In these scenarios, teams are usually not very effective, and none of the team members feel confident in their roles or get a chance to excel in their work.

The next time you find yourself in such a situation, instead of allowing the two different approaches to clash and compete, take a step back and ask yourself these questions:

1. What are my strengths underlying my approach?
2. What are my team member's strengths underlying his or her approach?
3. Could these strengths be used to complement each other? If not, could they at least be used in different areas?

If you have a willing team, go through these questions together or answer these questions on your own and share the results with your team. Suggest ways to apply each approach to different tasks, or take parts of each approach and put them together into a new approach.

TEACH WHAT YOU CAN DO

You might be familiar with the saying "If you can't do, teach!" While there are certainly teachers who reached for another career and fell back on teaching (and tend not to be great teachers), it's clear that this phrase does not apply to the majority of teachers. To teach something and teach it well, you have to really know your stuff.

This relationship also works in reverse: teaching something you know well can often take you from being merely competent to excelling in that area. Use this phenomenon to your advantage by teaching someone about your top strength.

You don't need to be a teacher, a professor, or a trainer to teach someone; all you need is a willing participant! A junior employee at your company is an excellent candidate for this volunteer position, but there are likely many people you know who would love to get a crash course, or even just a quick tutorial, in something you do well.

Teaching someone how to utilize a talent or skill that is one of your top strengths will help you get an even better grasp of it. In addition, teaching it will likely help you discover new areas to apply your strength and help you identify any gaps in your knowledge that you can fill in to improve your strength even further.

CHAPTER 9

EXERCISES TO INCREASE SELF-LOVE

One of the most important pieces of living a happy and healthy life is loving yourself. You've most likely heard the phrases "If you can't love yourself, how can you love anyone else?" or "If you can't love yourself, how can anyone else?" Of course, the implied meaning of these phrases is not entirely accurate, but there is a kernel of truth: it's hard to have healthy relationships with anyone else when you don't have a healthy relationship with yourself.

If you have struggled with showing yourself love, this is the perfect chapter for you. In the following pages, you will find exercises on how to boost your self-love and extend understanding, compassion, and forgiveness to yourself. Keep an open mind and give one or two of these exercises a try—it might just have a profound impact on how you relate to yourself and to others.

DIFFERENTIATE YOUR INNER CRITIC FROM YOUR AUTHENTIC SELF

A key step toward enhancing your self-compassion and self-love is acknowledging your inner critic. This may sound counterintuitive, but it really is very important to be able to determine when it is your inner critic speaking and when it is your optimistic and confident inner self speaking.

1. Grab your journal or notebook and open it to a fresh page. (If you don't have a journal or notebook, it's a good idea to go out and get one since many of the exercises in this chapter will call for using one.)
2. Draw a small self-portrait in the center of the page. Don't worry—it doesn't matter if it's good!
3. Next, draw several thought bubbles sprouting out from the portrait. In these thought bubbles, write down your most frequent negative thoughts about yourself. This might be a little painful, but try to push through it.
4. When you fill in all the bubbles, take a moment to recognize that all of these thoughts come from your inner critic. Label the portrait in the center "My Inner Critic."
5. Next, flip the page and do the exercise again, but with a focus on alternate ways to think about each bit of self-criticism. Label the portrait "My Authentic Self."

Whenever your negative thoughts start crowding out the good ones, return to these two pages to remind yourself that you are not your negative thoughts and that they do not need to define you.

GIVE THREE COMPLIMENTS

How often can you remember offering a friend or family member a compliment to cheer them up when they were feeling down? You probably do this all the time, without even thinking about it, to lift your loved one's spirits.

Now, how often do you offer *yourself* compliments to cheer yourself up and show yourself some love? Probably not very often (but kudos if you already do!). You may not think about it very often, but you have the power to compliment yourself and improve your day—the very same power you so often exercise when your friend's mood dips. To tap into this power and apply it to yourself, grab your journal or notebook and flip to a fresh page. Date the page and add the title "Three Compliments."

Next, jot down three genuine compliments to yourself. Are you having a good hair day? Do you feel particularly energetic today? Perhaps you did something nice that made someone feel good. If these examples apply to you, you might write compliments like:

* Your hair looks great today!
* You are bursting with energy and positive vibes.
* You're a really nice person.

This might feel awkward at first, especially if you're struggling with particularly low self-esteem, but keep at it! If the compliments are still not sinking in, try reading them out loud after you write them down. Eventually you will start to feel more positive about yourself.

START A POSITIVE FOCUS GROUP

This exercise may be the most difficult to do because it involves the commitment of several people; however, it is also one of the most impactful.

The positive focus group is a group activity that involves each member taking turns as the subject of a discussion of their strengths and positive qualities. Here's how you do it:

1. Enlist a group of friends and family members. If you have trouble getting people to agree to it, try reminding them that they will benefit from this exercise as well.
2. Set aside an hour or so (depending on how big your group is) and gather in a comfortable and private space, like someone's living room.
3. Choose someone to take the first turn, then engage in a discussion of everything you like about him or her: their strengths, their skills and talents, the qualities that make them a good friend or family member, or anything else you appreciate about them.
4. Continue the exercise with another group member, and repeat until each member has been the subject of the group's discussion.

If this sounds very uncomfortable to you, then you are probably one of those who stands to benefit the most from it! When you have low self-esteem and don't show yourself enough love, it's vital that you learn to recognize the good in yourself and believe in the positive things others say about you.

COMMIT TO THE EQUALITY PRINCIPLE

If someone asked you whether you believed that all people are equal, what would you say?

You would probably say yes to that question. Whether you find the principle of equality meaningful on a deeply personal level or you simply agree with the general idea, it's likely something that you believe in.

However, you've also probably had negative thoughts about yourself like "I'm not as good as him" or "They're so much better than I am" or even "I don't deserve to have what she has." Everyone has these thoughts at one point or another, but it's unhealthy to think them too often.

To neutralize these negative thoughts and shift how you see yourself, try committing to the Equality Principle wholeheartedly. The Equality Principle is the principle that we are all equally human and equally deserving of dignity, love, and happiness—including you!

On days when you're feeling particularly down, it might be tempting to make an exception for yourself, but remember that the Equality Principle has no exceptions. If everyone is deserving of love and happiness, you are deserving too.

If you're having trouble embracing this principle and accepting that there are no exceptions, try this technique: picture a dear friend or beloved family member and remind yourself that, since there are no exceptions, they are just as deserving of good things as you are. It's harder to keep up the negative thoughts when you have to apply them to someone you love!

TREAT YOURSELF LIKE A FRIEND

Paradoxically, one of the best ways to enhance your love and compassion for yourself is to imagine you are someone else! You will probably agree that it's much easier to forgive a friend's mistake or misstep than it is to forgive yourself that same transgression.

Putting yourself in the shoes of someone you love can help you to extend that same forgiveness and compassion to yourself.

When you notice yourself feeling down about a mistake you made, or beating yourself up for some perceived flaw, take a step back and pause your negative self-talk. Make a mental note of the things you are saying to yourself.

Now, imagine a close friend, beloved family member, or significant other is feeling the same way you are now. Think about how you would respond to your loved one. Make another mental note of the things you would say to him or her.

Next, compare the two dialogues. Did you find that your response to your loved one was significantly more compassionate than the response to yourself? If so, think about why you feel you deserve less compassion than your loved one.

Remind yourself that you are human and you make mistakes, just like your friend or family member, and you deserve the same forgiveness and compassion that you extend to those you love. If it helps, write this reminder down in a notebook or journal.

Repeat this exercise whenever you are being unnecessarily hard on yourself.

CREATE SELF-LOVE AFFIRMATIONS

You may have already come up with some affirmations to boost your confidence, but you can also come up with some affirmations to enhance your self-love. Follow these guidelines to create effective self-love affirmations:

1. Write your affirmations in the present tense. Focus on accepting yourself for who you are, right here and right now. Show yourself love in your current state.
2. Use a first-person perspective. Don't write statements about yourself as if you were someone else; write them from your own point of view.

Here are a few good examples of self-love affirmations:

* I am a good person.
* I am worthy of love and respect.
* I accept and love myself exactly as I am.

Repeat your affirmations at least once a day. It can be helpful to set a time of day for your affirmations to be sure you always remember to do them. Many people repeat their affirmations in the morning to get a boost of self-love for the rest of their day.

However, if you find yourself lagging in self-love at some point in your day, go ahead and repeat them again. Don't worry about overdoing it—you're in no danger of developing too much self-love!

GIVE YOURSELF A POSITIVE PEP TALK

It might sound silly, but the best way to neutralize negative self-talk is to use positive self-talk. Once you get over the awkwardness of talking to yourself in the mirror, you'll find that this exercise can work wonders for your self-love!

The next time you are feeling particularly down or negative about yourself, give this exercise a try.

1. Sit or stand in front of a mirror. Set a timer to make sure your positive pep talk lasts for at least 5 minutes.
2. To get started, look yourself in the eyes and give yourself a compliment. It might feel odd, but push through it! Give yourself another compliment. And another. Don't be surprised if the awkwardness wears off pretty quickly; it's easy to get the hang of positive self-talk!
3. Next, remind yourself of all your good qualities. List the things you're good at, and things you have done that you are proud of. Note some of your biggest accomplishments, and congratulate yourself on them.
4. Ask yourself whether, now that you've listed all the good things about yourself, you really believe in all the negative stuff your inner critic throws at you.
5. Finish by telling yourself that you are a good person and a person worthy of love and happiness.

Do this whenever you feel dragged down by your inner critic, and you will develop the ability to stop it in its tracks.

SET BOUNDARIES

One of the very best things you can do for yourself to enhance your sense of self-love is to set healthy boundaries. Setting boundaries can also help you in other areas as well, such as work and romantic relationships.

To set boundaries, try these steps:

1. Identify your limits. Think of situations as somewhere on a scale from 1 to 10, with 1 being *totally fine* and 10 being *totally distraught* or *unhappy*. Set your limit for situations at a 7.
2. Give yourself permission to say no to people. You need to get comfortable saying no to any situation at a 7 or higher, whether it's to your boss, your partner, or a needy friend.
3. Start asserting your boundaries on a small scale. Say no to something small, or something that isn't all that important to the requestor but would be unpleasant for you. Work your way up to the big things.
4. Practice being assertive and up-front. People will take your boundaries more seriously if you take them seriously, so sound like you mean it!

When you set boundaries, you are not only building healthier practices and better relationships, you are also building your self-respect. This a great way to prove to yourself that you are deserving, you are worthwhile, and you care about yourself.

FORGIVE YOURSELF

We have all done things we regret. You may have done something stupid, hurt someone, or made a poor decision for your own life—or you may have done all three, several times! No one is immune from mistakes, and we have all forgiven others for their mistakes, but it can sometimes be more difficult to extend our forgiveness to ourselves.

If you find it hard to forgive yourself and let go of the past, try these four steps:

1. Make a list of your biggest regrets. Don't include small things, like accidentally saying something insulting; these should be the regrets that weigh most heavily on you.
2. Accept that what you've done is in the past. This can be a very difficult step, but it's a vital one. Remind yourself that it can't be changed, and obsessing over it won't help anyone.
3. Imagine how you would have liked to handle the situation. Write this scenario down, and tell yourself that you won't make the same mistake going forward.
4. Remind yourself that change is a constant in life, and you are no longer the exact same person you were before.

Truly forgiving yourself and moving on will take time, but with practice, you can put your past behind you and move forward with a new sense of self-love and compassion.

LIST YOUR POSITIVE QUALITIES

When you're feeling down about yourself, sometimes all you need is a reminder of your good qualities. We all have at least a few good qualities, and listing them out can do wonders for our self-love.

Grab your journal or notebook and get ready to write a feel-good list!

Write "Good Things about Me" at the top of a page, and get to noting all of your positive qualities.

If you have trouble getting started, get the ball rolling by asking yourself, "What are my three favorite things about myself?" You might only be able to think of small things at first, like that you're good at crossword puzzles or you make some mean pancakes, but that's okay. As you go on, you'll think of your more important positive qualities.

If you still have trouble thinking of good things about yourself, imagine what someone who loves you would say. What does your mom like about you? What drew your spouse or significant other to you? What would your best friend say is his or her favorite thing about you?

Write down as many things as you can think of, and resist the urge to qualify them or explain them away (e.g., "He only thinks I'm good at public speaking because he's only seen me on my best days.").

Keep this list bookmarked in your journal and return to it whenever you're feeling down about yourself.

CELEBRATE YOUR SUCCESS

You have probably had a graduation party, a "congratulations on your new job" party, or some other kind of party celebrating something you accomplished. Remember how that felt? You had full permission to bask in the glow of your accomplishment, and it probably felt great! Celebrating your successes feels good and can make you feel more positively about yourself as well.

To take advantage of the boost in self-love you get from celebrating your achievements, it's simple—celebrate yourself more often! The next time you achieve or accomplish something, meet a goal, or just do something you are proud of, take some time to congratulate yourself and enjoy the moment.

Don't worry if it's not something huge; you don't have to wait for a big moment to celebrate yourself and revel in your success. Any little win will do!

* If you made good progress on one of your goals, celebrate!
* If you finished a difficult project at work, celebrate!
* If you made it to the gym at least three days this week— you guessed it, celebrate!

Celebrating your success, however large or small it feels, will show that you appreciate your own hard work and that you have reason to be proud of yourself. Do it as often as you can until you start feeling better about yourself.

LIST YOUR ACCOMPLISHMENTS

Reminding yourself of everything you have accomplished can go a long way toward boosting your love and compassion for yourself. To realize how many things you have actually accomplished, all you need is a pen and some paper.

If you have a journal or a diary, this is a great exercise to fill a page in it since you'll want to keep it for future reference.

At the top of the page, write "Awesome Things I Did" or some other title that captures your accomplishments.

Under the title, start listing all the awesome things you've done!

Don't worry if you need to list some "basic" things to get you started. You might not feel like it's a big deal if you graduated high school, but not everyone has! Go ahead and list it.

You can list things you've accomplished at work, like learning useful new skills or finishing a big project on time.

You can also note successes in your relationships, like staying with your significant other for five years or keeping your child healthy and well for ten years! Both of these are certainly accomplishments to be proud of.

Be sure to list any personal successes as well, like neutralizing an anger problem or successfully managing your anxiety.

When you really put your mind to it, you'll find that there are a million things you can list as accomplishments. Keep this list in your journal and turn to it whenever you need a reason to show yourself some love.

GIVE YOURSELF A LOVING TOUCH

We often show others we love them through touch. We give our friends and family members hugs, kiss them on the cheek, hold hands with our significant other, and give a back rub or neck massage when we're feeling especially generous.

This physical gesture of love can be extended to yourself as well as to those you love. The next time you are feeling upset, sad, or worried, soothe yourself with a loving touch.

Try any of the following touches, or go with whatever works best for you:

* Place one or both hands over your heart and rest them there for a few breaths.
* Give yourself a hug, placing your hands on your shoulders.
* Use one hand to gently hold the other.
* Stroke one arm with your opposite hand for a few minutes.
* Place a hand on each cheek and gently cradle your face.
* Wrap your arms around your belly and give a gentle squeeze.
* Run your hands through your hair or over your head in a gentle caress.
* Run your nails lightly down your neck and/or over your shoulders.

You may feel a little self-conscious at first, but these are all excellent ways to show yourself a little bit of love.

TRY SELF-LOVE MANTRAS

To carry your sense of self-love with you all day, wherever you go, try coming up with a mantra. Mantras are words, sets of phrases, or short sentences that help keep you focused on the things that matter to you. They are similar to affirmations, except affirmations are about boosting your self-love through self-acceptance. Mantras generally come from a "doing" perspective—they are focused on what you are capable of—while affirmations come from more of a "being" perspective.

When coming up with your mantra, follow these simple guidelines:

* Your mantra can be anywhere from one word to several sentences, but generally the shorter mantras are, the better.
* Your mantra should remind you of something you accomplished or something you are good at.
* Your mantra should make you feel good about yourself.

For example, if you are proud of your success in beating a drug addiction or healing from a major injury, you might choose a mantra like "I have overcome obstacles before. I will overcome obstacles again" or even just "Overcome."

Keep this mantra a secret tool for your use only, a special thing that you share only with yourself. Bring it out whenever you are struggling with fear, anxiety, anger, restlessness, or any other difficult situation or emotion, and allow it to remind you of where you've come from, where you've been, and where you're going.

CHAPTER 10

EXERCISES TO FACILITATE ACCEPTANCE

The name of this chapter may seem a bit vague to you; you might be thinking, "Exercises to facilitate the acceptance of what?" This chapter is about learning acceptance in general, but mainly it is about accepting two things: yourself, just as you are, and reality, just as it is.

Self-acceptance is vital to living a healthy and happy life. It's similar to self-esteem but centers on accepting, without judgment, the parts of yourself that you aren't so proud of or glad to have. Accepting reality is also a necessary component to living the good life. Humans are exceptionally good at denying reality when it doesn't fit their wants and needs, but this habit will not help you in the long run. If you're ready to work on accepting yourself and the reality of your situation, the exercises in this chapter will help you get started.

PRACTICE REFLECTIVE JOURNALING

This exercise is most effective when practiced every day, but doing it once in a while is better than nothing!

Buy yourself a notebook or journal to write in if you don't have one already. At the end of each day, note three things in your journal:

1. Write down at least one positive thing that happened to you or around you today. If you can think of more than one, don't stop there! Write as many good things as you'd like.

2. Write down a reflective question for yourself, but don't answer it yet. These questions should be grounded in your past experiences, your current life, or your hopes and dreams for the future; for example, you may write a question like "What truly made me happy this week?" or "What kind of person do I hope to be in one year?"

3. Reflect on the question you posed for yourself and come up with an answer for it. You don't need to write a comprehensive or definitive answer to this question, but you should put some time and effort into writing a substantive response that is authentically "you."

Practice this exercise every day (or as often as you can), and you will start to see a gradual improvement in your understanding and acceptance of yourself.

REPEAT SELF-ACCEPTANCE MANTRAS

Mantras are words, phrases, or sentences that you can use to keep yourself focused on what is most important to you. They are short statements you can say out loud or in your head to stay balanced and hang on to your desired perspective.

Mantras can be used for a wide variety of purposes and goals, but they are especially useful for facilitating self-acceptance.

To take advantage of the benefits mantras can bring, write down these four self-acceptance mantras and post them in a place where you can see them every day:

* I forgive myself for wrongs that I have done.
* I accept myself exactly as I am.
* I approve of myself exactly as I am.
* I love myself for who I am in this moment.

If none of these resonate with you, feel free to tweak them or come up with your own. Just make sure they affirm who you are in this very moment and with no qualifications or reservations.

Repeat these mantras at least once a day, but try to incorporate them into more of your day than just in the morning or at night. For example:

* When you're feeling down about yourself, repeat your mantras.
* When you make a mistake, repeat your mantras.
* When someone expresses their dissatisfaction or disappointment with you, repeat your mantras.

ADOPT AN ATTITUDE OF SELF-FORGIVENESS

To begin accepting yourself, it's important to learn how to forgive yourself—and not just once or twice for the big transgressions you have committed, but for everything you have done that you regret or feel guilty about.

Note that to forgive does not mean to condone. You can forgive yourself for anything you have done, no matter how awful you feel about it, without accepting that your behavior was good, right, or justified. Forgiving is not about believing your behavior is acceptable, but about accepting that it happened and deciding to move forward from it.

To start developing an attitude of self-forgiveness, keep a lookout for regrets and feelings of shame or guilt for past behaviors. Once one pops up, do the following:

1. Meet it head-on; accept that it happened.
2. Remind yourself that you did the best you could with the tools and knowledge available to you at the time.
3. Apologize to yourself (and, potentially, to anyone your actions affected) and *accept* your own apology.
4. Come up with a better way to handle any similar situations that arise in the future.
5. Commit to moving forward and leaving your guilt or shame in the past.

Repeat these steps for every regret that gnaws on your conscience, and you will be well on your way to developing an attitude of self-forgiveness.

ACCEPT YOUR DARK SIDE

As much as we might like to deny it, we all have a dark side. We all have urges that we would never act upon, and desires to do something illegal, unethical, or immoral. Even the saintliest human has at least once or twice had to deal with an urge to hurt someone or do something terrible.

A mistake that many of us make is to shun, deny, and repress this part of ourselves. It feels wrong to accept these kinds of thoughts and desires, but the alternative is even more damaging. True self-acceptance requires accepting even the darkest and most unpleasant aspects of yourself, even if you'd rather not acknowledge that they exist.

Paradoxically, when you accept that you have dark thoughts and urges, you gain greater control over them. This seems counterintuitive, but it's actually quite logical; if you don't accept that something exists, you give up any control or influence you may have over it. When you ignore it, you actually empower it.

Instead of ignoring your dark side, make an effort to accept it by following these steps:

1. Acknowledge the darker thoughts and urges you have.
2. Remind yourself that it's natural to have these thoughts and urges.
3. Assert your control over your behavior, no matter what thoughts and urges you have.

You will find that accepting your dark side and affirming that you have control over it is an empowering exercise.

COMMIT TO ACCEPTING WITHOUT IMPROVING

This is an exercise that many people struggle with; it can be hard enough to accept that you have flaws and make a plan to address them, but accepting your flaws without a plan to improve them is much more difficult.

Although we pay lip service to the idea that no one is perfect and we all have weaknesses and faults, many of us don't actually live this truth. Deep down, we expect ourselves to be perfect while forgiving others of their flaws, or have much higher standards for ourselves than for others.

Follow these guidelines to work on your ability to accept without improving:

1. Acknowledge that no one is perfect, and there is no expectation that you should be perfect.
2. Acknowledge that you have strengths and flaws, and list a few of each.
3. Tell yourself the following, out loud: "I have strengths and I have flaws, and that's okay."
4. Accept each strength and each flaw you noted with this declaration: "I accept that I am strong in [strength number one], and I accept that I am weak in [flaw number one]."
5. Finish by affirming the following, out loud: "I am okay with having strengths and flaws. I am okay just as I am."

Repeating these words can have a powerful effect on your self-acceptance, so don't be surprised if you feel emotional, exhilarated, or even liberated afterward.

USE STRATEGIC ACCEPTANCE

If you have trouble with the more traditional methods of acceptance, practicing strategic acceptance may be more effective for you.

Traditional methods of acceptance are all about accepting yourself and accepting reality because that's simply the way it is! These methods focus on acknowledging reality for what it is—not for any other motive, but because a fact is a fact.

If you are really struggling with your current situation or feeling exceptionally down about yourself, causing a lack of motivation to work on your self-acceptance, you might just need an ulterior motive to get you started.

When you practice strategic acceptance, you are getting to full acceptance in a roundabout way; you are using this ulterior motive to get yourself in the habit of acceptance, and after a while of practicing this way, you will eventually be able to shed the initial motive altogether.

To give strategic acceptance a try, simply read, repeat, and affirm this idea: "Accepting reality, exactly as it is, is the only way to protect myself against future undesirable situations like the one I'm in."

Once you find it easier to accept the situation you are in, even if you are only accepting it to try to change it in the future, slowly drop the ulterior motive and work toward accepting reality because it simply *is* reality.

GRIEVE FOR THE SELVES YOU HAVE LOST

The title of this exercise is not a typo! It sounds awkward, but it describes an important practice for enhancing your ability to accept yourself.

As children, we all have big dreams about what we will become; many of us are told that we can do anything we set our mind to, and that the sky is the limit! It's up for debate whether this is really true, but that is beyond the scope of this exercise.

Instead, this exercise is about remembering those big dreams you had as a child, adolescent, or young adult, and accepting that they may not come to fruition. This doesn't mean you should give up on your dream or resign yourself to never pursuing your passion; if you have a realistic shot at fulfilling a lifelong dream, go for it!

However, there are likely at least a few dreams or grand plans you hatched when you were younger that have already been derailed. The selves you have lost are the selves that you would have been, had these dreams worked out.

Identify these selves that never were and never will be, and grieve for them. Take some time to recognize that these dreams will never come true. Allow yourself to be sad for these missed opportunities.

Once you have grieved, put these unfulfilled dreams behind you and move forward. You can only work with what you've got, so commit to being your best self based on your reality and not your dreams.

TRY LOVING-KINDNESS MEDITATION

Loving-kindness meditation is a popular form of meditation that focuses on accepting yourself and others as they are, avoiding judgment, and extending compassion.

Take the following steps to give loving-kindness meditation a try:

1. Find a comfortable place to sit or lie down, and close your eyes.
2. Take a few deep, regular breaths to center yourself.
3. Think about a time when you did something good, something generous, or something kind. Offer yourself appreciation for this act.
4. Hold on to this feeling of appreciation, gratitude, and goodness, and extend it throughout your whole body. Send it all the way from your toes to the top of your head, from the tips of your fingers on your left hand all the way to the tips of your fingers on your right hand.
5. Once you feel this loving-kindness settle into your body, begin to extend it outside of yourself. Send it to those you love and those closest to you.
6. Next, send it to acquaintances.
7. Continue sending it out, all the way to people you don't particularly like and even people you hate.
8. Take the final step and send loving-kindness out to all beings. Extend this sense of acceptance, love, and compassion to every single person on earth and beyond.

ACCEPT THE STRUGGLE

Wouldn't it be nice if there was a maximum level of self-development you could reach, after which you had no need of development? You could simply work hard to attain this level of acceptance and transcendence, and suddenly everything would be clear. You would know how to deal with anything life threw your way, and nothing would ever drag you down again.

It sounds too good to be true because it *is* too good to be true. This is one of those facts that seems obvious but that we don't often live by; we might say that we know there is never a finish line for self-development, but we may still hold an ideal in our head of our perfectly rounded, completely developed, and unfailingly capable future self.

As nice as it is to hold this idea in your daydreams, you need to accept that your daydreams is where it must stay. Saying the following statements out loud will help you learn to accept their truth:

* I will never have everything figured out.
* I will always have something to learn.
* Struggles and hardship will always be a part of life.
* Pain is an unavoidable fact of life.

Once you have set these truths in your mind, finish off with the most important statement of all: "I will make it through."

Once you accept that struggling is a fact of life, you will be better equipped to handle it.

ACCEPT YOUR EMOTIONS

Accepting your emotions can be an extremely difficult thing to do, but it's vital for your health and happiness. It has been culturally ingrained in us that some emotions are unacceptable to show or even to feel, but this is like saying that it is unacceptable to catch a cold—you might not like it, but it is a fact of life and it can't be helped.

Learning to accept your emotions is a prerequisite for having a healthy sense of self-acceptance and self-love. It's often tempting to deny, reject, or repress your emotions, especially if they are not considered socially acceptable, but this will likely backfire. Emotions usually find a way to be expressed, whether they come out how you'd like to express them or they burst out in some other way!

Instead of letting your emotions bubble and eventually boil over, decide that you are going to accept them, and allow yourself to feel them. Acknowledge them, label them, and give yourself permission to have them.

You don't have much control over your emotions, but your actions do have an effect on how your emotions are experienced and expressed. Accepting that you have emotions, even those you'd rather not have, and allowing yourself to experience them as they come will free you from feeling controlled by them.

SEPARATE YOURSELF FROM YOUR EMOTIONS

It's vital to accept your emotions, but it can also be very helpful to separate yourself from them. The two exercises sound incompatible, but in reality, they're not mutually exclusive!

You have hundreds, if not thousands, of feelings every day. You are bombarded with instructions from your emotional brain on how to feel about everything on a moment-by-moment basis. You can easily get overwhelmed trying to process all of these emotions.

One option you have to keep balanced and in control is to separate yourself from your emotions. This can be especially helpful if you are feeling strong negative emotions, like sadness, anger, or anxiety.

To keep healthy boundaries between you and your emotions, remind yourself of the following:

* You are not your emotions. They are something you experience, not something you are.
* Your emotions do not dictate your behavior. You don't have a choice in how you feel, but you do have a choice in how you behave.
* You can feel your emotions without becoming them. Observe them, notice them, and acknowledge them, but let them pass by.

This exercise can help you keep control and accept yourself no matter what strong emotion you are experiencing.

DROP YOUR "SHOULDS"

Most of us live and breathe our "shoulds" all day long: we *should* go to the gym, we *shouldn't* get angry about that insult, we *should* be able to handle this, and so on. We are "shoulding" ourselves to death!

When you tell yourself you *should* do something, what you are really saying is that you should be a better person, meaning you are not acceptable as you are. It's great to have goals like getting to the gym five days a week, letting go of your anger, and feeling competent enough to handle issues; however, thinking of meeting these goals in terms of "should" instead of "will" can be destructive.

Instead of filling your head with admonishments about what you should or shouldn't do, ask yourself these questions to determine the best way to deal with your feelings about what you "should" do:

* Do I need to do this, or do I feel like I "should"?
* Do I want to do this, or do I feel like I "should"?

If it turns out you want or need to do it, then drop the "should" statement and stick with "want" or "need."

If you answer both questions with the "should" response, ask yourself why you feel that way. What is it that is making you feel like you *should* do something that you don't want or need to do?

Practice asking yourself these questions when you get sucked into thinking in terms of "shoulds," and you will quickly find that "should" statements don't have much power over you anymore.

ACCEPT YOUR VULNERABILITY

Being voluntarily vulnerable is one of the most difficult things you can do, but it's also one of the most rewarding. Without accepting vulnerability, you can never truly come to know yourself or to let yourself be known by others. Consequently, if you are never truly known, how can you be truly intimate with someone?

Aside from the importance of being vulnerable for happy, healthy relationships, fighting the feeling of being vulnerable only closes you up to self-discovery, self-acceptance, and self-love. Being vulnerable can be terrifying, but the benefits far outweigh the risks.

Take these steps to start accepting your vulnerability and opening yourself up to joy, pain, and everything in between:

* Acknowledge that you are worthy of love and happiness (some of the other exercises in this book can help with this step).
* Affirm that you have something valuable to offer to others.
* Accept that not everyone will like you, and know that that's okay.
* Commit to showing your real, authentic self to the people around you. If this sounds like a monumental task, start small—open yourself to one person at a time, and bit by bit.
* Decide that no matter what others think of you, you will not let their judgments affect how you feel about yourself.

ADJUST YOUR ATTITUDE ABOUT FAILURE

If you're terrified to fail or ashamed whenever you don't reach your highest goals, it's time for an attitude adjustment!

Failure is a fact of life. We all fail at some point, and you will fail too. This can be tough to accept, but think about the alternative: can you imagine going through life with every single thing working out perfectly and in your favor? No one would want to read that book or see that movie, because it's boring! It's also completely unattainable and unrealistic to boot.

Instead of fearing and shying away from failure, change your perspective on it. The next time you find yourself in a downward spiral about something that didn't work out right, read these statements about failure to yourself:

* Everybody fails, including me.
* Failure does not mean I am not good enough.
* Failure is not shameful or embarrassing; it means I was courageous and took a risk.
* If I never fail, I will never learn.
* "I failed" does not equal "I'm a failure."

Read through these statements and allow them to sink in. You might not feel like they're true, but keep reading through them until you start to accept them. Remind yourself of all the times some of the most successful people have failed (e.g., Steve Jobs, Walt Disney, Oprah Winfrey, Michael Jordan), and ask yourself whether failure is always such a bad thing. If you embrace failure as your teacher, it will not disappoint you.

INDEX